PYTHON SERVERLESS
FRAMEWORK FOR BEGINNERS

Mastering Python for Scalable, Cost-Effective Serverless

Applications

SIMON TELLIER

TABLE OF CONTENTS

PREFACE

Welcome to *Python Serverless Framework For Beginners: Mastering Python for Scalable, Cost-Effective Serverless Applications.* Whether you're a new developer or someone who has some experience with programming and is looking to explore the world of serverless computing, this book is for you. Serverless technology has grown exponentially in recent years, and it's become an invaluable tool for developers looking to create scalable, cost-effective applications without having to manage complex infrastructure.

With this book, you'll embark on a journey where you'll learn how to build serverless applications using Python, one of the most beginner-friendly and powerful programming languages available today. Python's ease of use, combined with serverless architecture, opens the door to developing highly efficient applications in a fraction of the time it would take with traditional cloud infrastructure. If you've ever felt bogged down by server maintenance or complex setup requirements, serverless computing will revolutionize how you approach building apps.

Through clear explanations, hands-on projects, and real-world examples, this book will guide you step by step in mastering Python's role in serverless frameworks, particularly with AWS Lambda. You won't just learn theory—this book is designed for those who prefer practical, interactive learning. By the end of this book, you'll have the skills to create scalable and cost-effective serverless applications and take your development abilities to the next level.

Let's get started!

Introduction to the Book

The way we build applications is changing. Cloud services, especially those that offer serverless computing, have introduced an entirely new paradigm that allows developers to focus on writing code rather than managing the infrastructure it runs on. Whether you're building web apps, mobile backends, or data-processing pipelines, the serverless approach simplifies deployment and dramatically reduces the overhead associated with running servers.

Serverless refers to a cloud computing model where the cloud provider manages the infrastructure for you. In this model, you simply upload your code, and the cloud platform takes care of provisioning, scaling, and managing the servers required to run it. This has proven to be highly efficient, as it helps developers avoid worrying about server configuration, capacity planning, and uptime. Instead, they can focus purely on developing the features that matter.

When we add Python into the mix, things get even more exciting. Python is not only incredibly popular but also highly versatile. It's known for its readability and simplicity, making it an excellent choice for beginners. Python works seamlessly with the serverless framework, and in this book, you'll explore how Python interacts with AWS Lambda and other services, which are foundational to building serverless applications.

This book will cover the essential concepts, tools, and techniques you need to build your first Python-based serverless application. By the end of this book, you'll be confident in your ability to leverage Python in a serverless context, and you'll have the practical experience needed to create your own fully functional applications using AWS services like Lambda, API Gateway, and DynamoDB.

Who This Book Is For

This book is tailored for individuals who are looking to dive into serverless computing with Python, regardless of their background or experience. If you're a beginner in Python or serverless architecture, this book will guide you through the fundamentals, gradually building up your knowledge so you can feel comfortable working on real-world projects.

This book is also for experienced developers who may already have some familiarity with serverless computing or Python but want to deepen their understanding and learn how to apply Python to serverless architectures effectively.

Here's a breakdown of who will benefit most from this book:

1. **Beginners in Python Programming**
   If you're just starting to learn Python, this book is a great place to begin your journey into serverless computing. While some basic understanding of Python is helpful, the book will ensure that you learn the language fundamentals you'll need along the way. We'll start with easy-to-understand examples and build on them as we go.

2. **Newcomers to Serverless Computing**
   If you're unfamiliar with the term "serverless" or the concept behind it, don't worry! This book will break down the fundamental concepts in a way that anyone can understand, even if you have no prior experience with cloud technologies. Serverless is one of the hottest trends in the tech industry, and this book will show you how it works, why it's useful, and how to build serverless apps using Python.

3. **Experienced Developers Exploring Serverless**

   If you're an experienced developer, especially someone who's familiar with AWS services or cloud technologies, this book will teach you how to take full advantage of Python within a serverless framework. You'll be able to use the lessons to apply serverless architecture to your current or future projects, speeding up your development process and minimizing infrastructure headaches.

4. **Tech Entrepreneurs and Startups**

   Serverless architecture is perfect for tech entrepreneurs and startups because it allows you to rapidly build scalable applications without the need for expensive infrastructure. If you have a great app idea but limited resources to build and maintain servers, this book will show you how to develop scalable and cost-effective applications quickly, even with a small team or as a solo developer.

5. **Anyone Interested in Cost-Effective Cloud Solutions**

   Serverless applications are often cheaper to run than traditional cloud applications because you only pay for what you use. If you're looking to build an app with minimal upfront costs or reduce cloud service bills, this book will show you how to achieve that using AWS Lambda and Python.

This book is perfect for anyone who wants to harness the power of serverless architecture using Python, whether you're just getting started with programming or you're an experienced developer looking to build scalable, cost-effective applications without dealing with the complexities of traditional cloud setups.

So, if you're ready to start building powerful serverless applications with Python, this book is your gateway to that world.

What You Will Learn

In this book, you'll gain practical, hands-on experience with Python and serverless computing. By the time you finish, you'll not only understand the concepts but also be able to build and deploy serverless applications using Python. Here's a look at what you can expect to learn:

1. **Serverless Computing Fundamentals**
   o What serverless computing is, and how it differs from traditional cloud computing.
   o The key benefits of serverless architecture, such as cost savings, scalability, and ease of management.
   o The core components of a serverless application, such as functions, APIs, and databases, and how they fit together.

2. **Introduction to AWS Lambda and Python**
   o How AWS Lambda works and why it's an excellent platform for serverless applications.
   o How Python is integrated with AWS Lambda, and how to write Lambda functions in Python.
   o The basics of deploying serverless Python applications to AWS Lambda.

3. **Hands-On Projects and Real-World Examples**
   o Building serverless applications from scratch using Python.
   o Creating REST APIs with AWS API Gateway and Python Lambda functions.
   o Working with databases, including DynamoDB, to store and retrieve data in a serverless environment.
   o Practical examples such as building a serverless contact form and a chatbot using AWS Lex and Lambda.

4. **Cost Management and Optimization in Serverless Architectures**
   o How AWS Lambda pricing works, and how to keep your costs under control.
   o Cost-saving tips for optimizing function execution time and memory usage.

- Monitoring and optimizing your serverless applications to ensure you're running efficiently.

5. **Security Best Practices for Serverless Applications**
   - How to secure your serverless applications and Lambda functions using IAM roles and permissions.
   - Ensuring data security when using AWS services, including data encryption and secure APIs.
   - Protecting your applications against common security threats in serverless environments.

6. **Debugging and Troubleshooting Serverless Applications**
   - How to debug Lambda functions and monitor them using AWS CloudWatch.
   - Identifying and resolving common errors and performance bottlenecks in serverless applications.
   - Using logging and tracing to track the behavior of serverless functions.

7. **Scaling and Performance Optimization**
   - How serverless applications scale automatically with demand.
   - Optimizing performance to reduce latency and speed up function execution times.
   - Advanced scaling strategies using Lambda, API Gateway, and DynamoDB.

8. **Advanced Serverless Patterns**
   - Creating serverless microservices and event-driven architectures.
   - How to handle state management in serverless applications with AWS Step Functions.
   - Advanced patterns like serverless machine learning using Lambda and Python.

9. **Continuous Integration and Deployment (CI/CD) for Serverless**
   - Setting up a continuous deployment pipeline for serverless applications.

6

- ○ Automating testing and deployment of Lambda functions using AWS SAM (Serverless Application Model).
- ○ Integrating with tools like GitHub Actions or AWS CodePipeline for smooth deployments.

10. **The Future of Serverless and Python**

- Exploring the future of serverless technologies and how Python is evolving to support these innovations.
- Other serverless platforms beyond AWS, such as Google Cloud Functions or Azure Functions.
- How serverless computing is changing the landscape of application development and what it means for developers.

How to Use This Book

This book is designed to be a **practical guide**, so the best way to use it is to follow along and work through the examples and projects as you go. Here's how you can make the most of it:

1. **Start from the Beginning**
   If you're new to serverless computing or Python, it's a good idea to start from the first chapter and work through the book sequentially. Each chapter builds on the last, so following the flow will ensure you have a solid understanding before moving on to more advanced topics.

2. **Follow the Hands-On Projects**
   This book is designed to help you learn by doing. At the end of many chapters, you'll find hands-on projects that put the concepts into practice. These projects are structured in a way that helps you apply the skills you've just learned, and by the end, you'll have created a fully functioning serverless application.

3. **Experiment and Modify Examples**

   As you work through the examples, don't hesitate to experiment and modify the code to suit your own needs. Serverless computing offers a lot of flexibility, and Python is incredibly adaptable, so you'll likely find that tweaking the examples will help you learn even more. The more you experiment, the better your understanding will become.

4. **Refer Back to Key Sections**

   Some chapters cover advanced topics like cost optimization, performance tuning, and debugging. If you ever run into issues while building your own serverless applications, feel free to go back and refer to these sections. There's no need to read everything at once—use the book as a reference guide when needed.

5. **Utilize the Companion GitHub Repository**

   Many of the projects and code examples in this book will be available on a **companion GitHub repository**. This will allow you to easily access the code, follow along with the examples, and check out the solutions to projects. We encourage you to clone the repository and use it to practice building your own serverless applications.

6. **Work at Your Own Pace**

   Whether you're a beginner or an experienced developer, take your time with the book. If you're new to serverless computing, don't rush through the chapters. It's important to grasp the concepts and not just copy the code. On the other hand, if you already have experience with serverless, feel free to skip ahead to the more advanced chapters or focus on the sections that interest you most.

7. **Join the Community**

   Consider joining the online community of learners, developers, and practitioners who are working with serverless technologies. Participate in forums, read blogs, and ask questions about what you're building. Serverless technology is constantly evolving, and connecting with others can help you stay up to date on new trends and practices.

8. **Keep Practicing and Building**

   As with any new skill, the key to mastering serverless development with Python is **practice**. After finishing this book, continue to build your own serverless applications. Push yourself to try new things, tackle new challenges, and develop more sophisticated projects. The more you build, the more you'll be able to create innovative, scalable, and cost-effective solutions.

By the end of this book, you'll be ready to tackle real-world serverless projects, whether you're building your own applications or working on enterprise-level systems. The journey from understanding serverless basics to deploying and scaling serverless applications is a rewarding one, and we're excited to guide you through it.

Chapter 1: Introduction to Serverless Computing

Serverless computing is transforming how developers approach application design and deployment. In this chapter, we'll break down what serverless architecture is, how it differs from traditional computing models, and the significant benefits it offers to developers. By the end of this chapter, you'll have a clear understanding of serverless computing and why it's becoming an increasingly popular choice for building modern applications.

What is Serverless Architecture?

At its core, **serverless architecture** allows developers to build and run applications without managing the infrastructure. Traditionally, developers had to provision servers, manage their configurations, and scale them manually to handle varying levels of traffic. With serverless computing, this responsibility is shifted to the cloud provider (like AWS, Azure, or Google Cloud), which automatically manages infrastructure scaling, availability, and resource allocation.

Despite the name, serverless doesn't mean there are no servers involved—it simply means that the server management and maintenance are taken care of by the cloud provider, so developers don't need to worry about them. Instead, developers can focus on writing the code that powers the application and let the provider take care of scaling, maintaining uptime, and handling failures.

In serverless computing, developers create small units of execution called **functions**, which are triggered by events. These functions are stateless, meaning they don't retain information between executions. The cloud provider takes care of scaling these functions as needed, ensuring that resources are allocated based on demand. This makes serverless applications highly scalable, cost-effective, and efficient.

One of the most well-known implementations of serverless computing is **AWS Lambda**, which allows you to run your code in response to events, such as HTTP requests, file uploads, or database changes. However, other cloud providers like Google Cloud Functions and Azure Functions offer similar serverless solutions.

Benefits of Going Serverless

The shift to serverless computing provides numerous advantages, making it a compelling choice for many developers and businesses. Here are some of the key benefits:

1. **Cost Efficiency**

   One of the most significant advantages of serverless computing is its **cost efficiency**. In traditional server setups, you must provision and pay for servers, even if they aren't being used at full capacity. With serverless, you only pay for the actual compute time your functions consume. If your function isn't being called, you don't incur any costs. This "pay-as-you-go" model allows businesses to reduce infrastructure costs significantly.

   Moreover, serverless providers typically offer a free tier for usage, which is especially beneficial for small applications or startups. AWS Lambda, for instance, provides 1 million free requests and 400,000 GB-seconds of compute time per month, allowing developers to experiment without worrying about costs.

2. **Scalability**

   Serverless architecture automatically scales to meet the demand of your application. When an event occurs (e.g., an HTTP request, a new file uploaded to storage, or a database update), the serverless platform automatically provisions the necessary resources to run the associated function. If traffic spikes, more instances of the function are created to handle the load, and when demand decreases, the platform scales down resources accordingly.

This ability to **scale on demand** without manual intervention ensures that serverless applications can handle varying workloads with ease. Developers don't need to worry about over-provisioning or under-provisioning resources, making the system both reliable and cost-effective.

3. **No Server Management**

One of the key benefits of serverless computing is that you don't need to manage or maintain servers. In traditional models, developers are responsible for provisioning, scaling, and patching the servers, which takes time and expertise. With serverless, the cloud provider takes care of these tasks, allowing developers to focus on writing and deploying code.

By removing the need for server maintenance, developers can save time and avoid many of the headaches associated with managing infrastructure. This enables them to deliver features faster and spend more time improving the application rather than managing the underlying infrastructure.

4. **Improved Developer Productivity**

Serverless architecture simplifies many of the operational aspects of development, such as scaling, monitoring, and server management. With these responsibilities handled by the cloud provider, developers can focus more on writing business logic and improving features. This leads to faster development cycles and quicker time-to-market for new applications and features.

Additionally, serverless allows for rapid prototyping and experimentation. Developers can quickly deploy individual functions, test them in production, and iterate based on feedback. This improves agility and accelerates the development process.

5. **Built-in Availability and Fault Tolerance**

Serverless providers typically offer built-in **availability** and **fault tolerance** as part of their offerings. Because serverless functions are run in the cloud, they are inherently highly available. If a function fails or an error occurs, the cloud provider can automatically retry the function or route the request to another instance of the function, ensuring the system remains resilient.

Many cloud providers also ensure that their serverless platforms are geographically distributed, so functions are executed on servers in multiple locations. This **multi-region deployment** improves the reliability and availability of applications.

6. **Automatic Scaling of Infrastructure**

   With traditional infrastructure, scaling to handle an increase in traffic requires manual intervention, such as adding new servers, load balancers, or database clusters. With serverless computing, the cloud provider automatically scales your functions in response to demand, so you don't need to worry about how to handle more users or traffic.

   For example, when a large number of requests come in, AWS Lambda automatically adds more instances of your function to process the requests concurrently. As traffic decreases, it scales down the number of instances, so you're never paying for unused resources.

7. **Faster Time to Market**

   By leveraging serverless platforms, development teams can push updates and new features faster than traditional infrastructure allows. With fewer infrastructure concerns to manage, the focus shifts to building features and improving the application's performance. Serverless architectures facilitate a more streamlined deployment process, leading to faster releases and updates.

8. **Enhanced Security**

   Security is a critical concern for any application, and serverless computing helps address this in several ways. Serverless providers offer built-in security features, such as automatic encryption of data in transit and at rest, secure connections between services, and fine-grained access control through IAM (Identity and Access Management) roles.

   Serverless functions are isolated from one another, meaning that if one function is compromised, the rest of the application remains unaffected. Additionally, the cloud provider's security team handles many of the security updates and patches, ensuring that the platform is always up to date.

Serverless computing is revolutionizing the way developers approach application development and infrastructure management. By eliminating the need for manual server provisioning and scaling, serverless architecture allows developers to focus on writing code and creating new features, all while benefiting from automatic scaling, cost efficiency, and built-in availability. This paradigm shift offers significant advantages, including reduced infrastructure costs, faster development cycles, and improved scalability, making it an attractive option for both new and experienced developers alike.

Next, we'll dive deeper into the specifics of why Python is such an excellent choice for serverless computing and how it integrates seamlessly with cloud platforms like AWS Lambda. Whether you're a seasoned developer or just getting started, Python's simplicity and flexibility will make your journey into serverless architecture smooth and efficient.

Serverless vs Traditional Cloud Computing

To understand serverless computing, it's essential to compare it with traditional cloud computing models. While both approaches use cloud infrastructure, the way resources are managed, scaled, and billed is different. Let's break down the key distinctions between serverless and traditional cloud computing:

1. **Resource Management**
   - **Traditional Cloud Computing:** In traditional cloud environments (such as Virtual Machines or Infrastructure as a Service - IaaS), you are responsible for provisioning and managing the underlying infrastructure. You need to decide on the number of virtual machines (VMs) or servers

required to run your application, configure load balancing, and manage the scaling of those resources.

- o **Serverless Computing:** With serverless, you don't have to worry about provisioning or managing servers. You upload your code, define its triggers (such as an HTTP request or a file upload), and the cloud provider takes care of the rest. Resources scale automatically based on demand without manual intervention.

2. **Scalability**
   - o **Traditional Cloud Computing:** Scalability in traditional cloud environments is handled manually. You have to decide in advance how many servers or VMs you need, which can lead to underutilization or over-provisioning. If your application's traffic increases, you need to adjust the infrastructure by adding more servers, which can take time.
   - o **Serverless Computing:** Serverless automatically scales based on the demand. For example, if an event triggers multiple requests at once, the cloud provider will spin up more instances of your function to handle the load. When traffic drops, it will automatically scale down. This automatic scaling is one of the key benefits of serverless computing, as it ensures your application can handle spikes in demand without manual intervention.

3. **Cost Efficiency**
   - o **Traditional Cloud Computing:** In traditional cloud environments, you typically pay for the server instances you provision, regardless of how much they're used. Even if your servers are idle most of the time, you're still paying for the allocated resources.
   - o **Serverless Computing:** With serverless, you pay only for the actual compute time your functions consume. This "pay-as-you-go" model ensures that you only pay for the resources used during function execution, making it much more cost-effective, especially for

applications with variable traffic or those that don't need to run constantly.

4. **Infrastructure Maintenance**

   - **Traditional Cloud Computing:** With traditional cloud models, you are responsible for managing the infrastructure—setting up servers, configuring operating systems, applying security patches, and monitoring system performance. This can take significant time and effort, particularly as your application scales.

   - **Serverless Computing:** Serverless platforms abstract away infrastructure management. The cloud provider is responsible for provisioning and maintaining the underlying hardware, operating systems, and runtime environments. Developers can focus solely on writing the business logic for their application rather than worrying about maintaining servers.

5. **Development Speed and Agility**

   - **Traditional Cloud Computing:** While cloud computing still accelerates development compared to on-premise infrastructure, the need to manage servers, scaling, and other infrastructure tasks can slow down the development process, especially when manual intervention is required.

   - **Serverless Computing:** Serverless architecture speeds up development by allowing you to focus on writing code. Serverless functions are event-driven and can be developed, deployed, and updated quickly. Developers can iterate faster, deploy smaller units of work, and experiment with features without worrying about the infrastructure.

Key Components of Serverless Applications

A serverless application typically consists of several key components that work together to deliver a fully functional, event-driven system. Let's explore each of these components:

1. **Functions**

   The fundamental unit of a serverless application is the **function**. In serverless computing, functions are small, stateless blocks of code that are triggered by events. These functions are executed in response to specific actions, such as an HTTP request, a file upload, or a change in a database. Functions are typically short-lived and are designed to perform specific tasks.

   Example: A function might be triggered when a user uploads an image to cloud storage, and its task could be to resize the image and store the resized version.

2. **Event Sources**

   In serverless computing, events are the triggers that invoke serverless functions. An event can come from a variety of sources, such as HTTP requests, database changes, file uploads, or even changes in cloud storage. These events are used to trigger the execution of functions, making serverless applications highly event-driven.

   Example: An HTTP request to an API endpoint or an update to a record in a DynamoDB table could trigger a function. The serverless framework listens for these events and executes the appropriate functions when needed.

3. **API Gateway**

   An **API Gateway** is a key component for building serverless applications, especially when you're dealing with web applications or mobile backends. The API Gateway is responsible for routing requests from clients to the appropriate serverless functions. It acts as a reverse proxy, handling HTTP requests and forwarding them to the correct function based on the endpoint and method specified.

   Example: AWS API Gateway can be used to expose HTTP endpoints that trigger AWS Lambda functions. This enables developers to build RESTful APIs without managing traditional servers.

4. **Databases and Storage**

   Serverless applications often rely on cloud-based storage and databases to persist data. **Serverless databases**, like **AWS DynamoDB**, provide automatic scaling and high availability without requiring manual provisioning or management. You can easily connect serverless functions to databases and storage systems to store and retrieve data.

Example: A serverless function might interact with DynamoDB to store user information or query a database for specific data. Similarly, cloud storage services like Amazon S3 are commonly used to store files like images or documents.

5. **Identity and Access Management (IAM)**

   IAM plays a crucial role in securing serverless applications. It controls who can access serverless functions, API endpoints, and other cloud resources. By defining IAM roles and permissions, you can enforce security policies and ensure that only authorized users or services can invoke functions or access sensitive data.

   Example: An IAM role might be assigned to a Lambda function to grant it the necessary permissions to interact with DynamoDB or S3, while ensuring that other functions or users do not have unnecessary access.

6. **Event Bus and Message Queues**

   Serverless applications often rely on event-driven patterns, where different parts of the system communicate asynchronously through events. **Event buses** and **message queues** allow different components of your serverless architecture to communicate with each other.

   Example: AWS EventBridge is an event bus service that allows you to build event-driven applications. AWS SQS (Simple Queue Service) is a message queue service that can be used to decouple different parts of a serverless application, allowing them to process messages asynchronously.

Chapter 2: Why Python for Serverless Applications

When it comes to developing serverless applications, the choice of programming language plays a crucial role in the efficiency, scalability, and ease of development. While there are many languages that can be used with serverless frameworks, Python stands out as one of the best options, especially when paired with platforms like AWS Lambda. In this chapter, we'll explore why Python is an ideal language for building serverless applications and how it works seamlessly with AWS Lambda.

The Strengths of Python: Why Choose It for Serverless

Python has been a popular programming language for years, and it continues to be favored by developers for various reasons. Here are some of the key strengths of Python that make it a great choice for serverless computing:

1. **Simplicity and Readability**
   Python is widely regarded for its **clean syntax** and **readability**, making it an ideal language for both beginners and experienced developers. The language is designed to be easy to understand and write, with clear and concise code that reduces the complexity of development. This is particularly beneficial in serverless environments, where rapid prototyping and quick deployment are essential. Python's simplicity also means that developers can focus on business logic rather than battling with complex syntax.
   Additionally, Python's **indented structure** encourages developers to write code that is well-organized and easy to maintain, which is crucial when dealing with the distributed nature of serverless applications.

2. **Extensive Library Support**

   One of Python's standout features is its vast **standard library** and the extensive collection of third-party libraries available. The Python Package Index (PyPI) contains over 200,000 libraries, covering a wide range of functionalities, from web frameworks (like Flask and Django) to machine learning (TensorFlow, scikit-learn) and data processing (Pandas, NumPy).

   This extensive library support means that Python developers can leverage pre-built functions and tools to quickly build out serverless applications. Whether you need to interact with databases, process files, or build APIs, Python's libraries offer everything you need to get started.

3. **Versatility and Flexibility**

   Python is an incredibly versatile language. It's used for everything from web development and data science to automation and machine learning. This versatility means that it can handle a wide variety of tasks in serverless computing. Whether you're building a simple API, a real-time data processing pipeline, or a machine learning-powered application, Python can do it all.

   The flexibility of Python also makes it a great choice for **multifunctional serverless applications**. It can work with a variety of AWS services like Lambda, S3, API Gateway, DynamoDB, and more, enabling you to build complex, distributed systems without worrying about language compatibility.

4. **Fast Development and Prototyping**

   Python's simplicity and the availability of powerful libraries make it an excellent language for quickly developing and prototyping applications. When you build serverless applications, especially in startups or small teams, **time to market** is crucial. Python's concise syntax allows you to get projects up and running quickly. In fact, it's often cited as one of the best languages for rapid prototyping, which is a significant advantage in fast-paced environments.

   In serverless development, you can take advantage of Python's speed in both development and execution to rapidly iterate on your application, experiment with new ideas, and deliver features faster.

5. **Community and Ecosystem**

   Python has a vibrant and active community of developers, which means that you have access to a wealth of knowledge, tutorials, open-source projects, and forums. The Python community actively contributes to its growth, ensuring that Python continues to evolve with the needs of developers.

   In addition to the community, Python has strong ecosystem support for cloud platforms like AWS, Azure, and Google Cloud. Tools like **AWS SAM (Serverless Application Model)** and the **Serverless Framework** have first-class support for Python, making it easy to integrate Python with AWS Lambda and other serverless services.

6. **Performance for Serverless Computing**

   While Python is not the fastest language in terms of raw performance (compared to languages like C++ or Go), it is **fast enough** for most serverless use cases, especially given its ease of development and flexibility. Many serverless applications do not require ultra-low-latency execution, and Python performs well within the constraints of serverless functions.

   Additionally, Python's performance can be enhanced by taking advantage of **multi-threading** and **asynchronous programming**. This allows Python to efficiently handle concurrent tasks, such as making multiple API requests or processing multiple data streams in parallel.

Python and AWS Lambda: A Perfect Match

AWS Lambda is the most popular serverless platform, and it has excellent support for Python. AWS Lambda allows you to run Python functions in response to events, without needing to manage any servers. Here's why Python and AWS Lambda are a perfect match:

1. **Ease of Integration with AWS Services**

   AWS Lambda natively supports Python, allowing developers to create serverless functions using Python code that can interact with a variety of AWS services, such as S3, DynamoDB, API Gateway, and more. This integration is incredibly seamless, enabling you to build scalable, event-driven applications without having to worry about complex infrastructure.

   Lambda functions written in Python can be triggered by a wide range of events, from HTTP requests to changes in DynamoDB tables or new files uploaded to S3. This makes it easy to build a fully integrated system with minimal setup.

2. **Lambda's Lightweight Execution Environment**

   AWS Lambda functions are designed to run in a **lightweight, ephemeral environment**. This is a great fit for Python because the language's dependencies are generally small and easy to package into deployment packages. Python's rapid execution and lightweight nature make it ideal for serverless functions, where you want to minimize the overhead of each invocation.

   AWS Lambda's execution environment also supports Python's asynchronous capabilities, which is a huge benefit for Python developers who need to handle I/O-bound tasks, such as network requests, database queries, or file processing, concurrently.

3. **Quick Cold Start Times**

   Cold starts occur when a Lambda function is triggered for the first time (or after it's been idle for a while), and AWS needs to initialize the function's execution environment. While cold start times can be an issue for some languages, Python generally has fast cold start times due to its lightweight nature. This is particularly important in serverless computing, where latency can impact user experience.

   With AWS Lambda, you can minimize cold starts by optimizing your function's initialization, leveraging the inherent speed of Python, and ensuring that your code is lean and only includes necessary dependencies.

4. **Seamless Deployment and Management**

   AWS Lambda allows you to deploy Python functions easily using the AWS Management Console, AWS CLI, or Infrastructure-as-Code tools like **AWS CloudFormation** and **AWS SAM** (Serverless Application Model). Python's simplicity allows you to quickly package your code, define triggers, and deploy your serverless function in a matter of minutes.

   Additionally, AWS provides robust tools for monitoring and logging, such as **AWS CloudWatch**, which allows you to track function invocations, debug errors, and optimize performance. Python's integration with CloudWatch makes it easy to capture logs from Lambda functions and use them for troubleshooting and performance tuning.

5. **Event-Driven Programming with AWS Lambda**

   Serverless computing is inherently **event-driven**, meaning that actions (events) trigger specific responses (functions). Python is particularly well-suited to event-driven programming, thanks to its clear and concise syntax. Lambda functions written in Python respond to various events such as HTTP requests via API Gateway, database changes in DynamoDB, file uploads to S3, or messages in SQS (Simple Queue Service). This event-driven model makes Python a natural choice for Lambda-based serverless applications.

6. **Cost-Effective for Python Serverless Functions**

   AWS Lambda's pricing model is based on the **number of requests** and **execution time**, meaning you only pay for the compute time you use. Python is an efficient language that tends to consume fewer resources for typical serverless tasks, which helps keep costs low. In many cases, Python's quick execution time and minimal resource consumption translate into **lower operational costs**, making it an ideal choice for building cost-effective serverless applications.

Python's simplicity, vast library ecosystem, and versatility make it an excellent choice for serverless applications. Whether you are building APIs, processing real-time data, or integrating with other cloud services, Python enables you to rapidly develop and deploy serverless functions. Pairing Python with AWS Lambda only enhances its power, offering a highly scalable, cost-effective, and efficient way to build modern applications. Next, we will guide you through the process of setting up your development environment and starting with AWS Lambda and Python, so you can begin building your own serverless applications right away.

Overview of Python's Libraries for Serverless Development

One of the key reasons Python excels in serverless development is its extensive library ecosystem. Libraries are pre-written chunks of code that help developers avoid reinventing the wheel. With the right libraries, serverless development becomes much more manageable and efficient. In this section, we'll highlight some of the essential Python libraries for building serverless applications and how they integrate with AWS Lambda and other cloud services.

1. **Boto3 - The AWS SDK for Python**
   One of the most essential libraries for working with AWS services in Python is **Boto3**. Boto3 is the AWS SDK (Software Development Kit) for Python, and it provides an interface for interacting with AWS services like **Lambda, S3, DynamoDB, SQS, SNS**, and many more. With Boto3, you can manage AWS resources directly from your Python code, making it a key tool for serverless developers.
   - **Example Use Cases:**
     - Interacting with DynamoDB to store or retrieve data.
     - Triggering Lambda functions programmatically.
     - Uploading files to S3 or retrieving files from an S3 bucket.
     - Sending messages to SQS queues or SNS topics.
2. Boto3 abstracts much of the complexity of interacting with AWS, making it simple to integrate AWS services into your serverless applications.

3. **AWS Lambda Powertools for Python**

   AWS Lambda Powertools is a set of utilities that simplify common tasks in Lambda functions. It's an open-source library developed by AWS, and it helps you write cleaner, more efficient serverless applications with Python. Some of its key features include:

   - **Structured Logging:** Automatically formats logs in JSON, making them easier to parse and analyze.
   - **Metrics and Tracing:** Integrates with AWS CloudWatch for better monitoring and observability.
   - **Middleware:** Provides a way to add reusable logic to Lambda functions, such as validation, authentication, and error handling.

4. This library is ideal for those building production-grade serverless applications where monitoring, debugging, and maintainability are important.

5. **Zappa**

   Zappa is a powerful Python library designed to make it easy to deploy Python web applications (including those built with frameworks like Flask and Django) to AWS Lambda. Zappa abstracts the complexities of deploying Python apps to AWS Lambda and API Gateway, making it an excellent choice for serverless web applications. It handles API Gateway integration, function deployment, and auto-scaling.

   - **Example Use Cases:**
     - Deploying a web app built with Flask or Django to AWS Lambda.
     - Automatically handling deployments and scaling of web applications.
     - Serving static files through AWS S3 while using Lambda for dynamic content.

6. **Serverless Framework (Python Integration)**

   While the Serverless Framework itself is not Python-specific, it offers a powerful way to deploy serverless applications using Python. The **Serverless Framework** provides a declarative way to define Lambda functions, API Gateway routes, and other resources in a simple YAML configuration file. With Python integration, you can write your Lambda functions in Python, deploy them to AWS, and manage your serverless infrastructure with ease.

- **Example Use Cases:**
  - Managing Lambda functions and other AWS resources declaratively with YAML.
  - Handling deployments, versioning, and environment variables with ease.
  - Integrating with AWS services like API Gateway, DynamoDB, and S3.

7. The Serverless Framework simplifies serverless application development and is highly recommended for developers looking to streamline their deployment process.

8. **Flask and FastAPI for Building Serverless APIs**

   Flask is a popular micro-framework for Python that makes it easy to build web applications and APIs. While Flask itself is not serverless, it's commonly used in serverless applications with AWS Lambda to create REST APIs. AWS Lambda, when paired with **AWS API Gateway**, can serve Flask-based web applications in a serverless environment.

   FastAPI is a modern, fast (high-performance), web framework for building APIs with Python based on standard Python type hints. It's designed for building APIs quickly and efficiently, and it also works well in serverless applications, making it an excellent alternative to Flask.

   - **Example Use Cases:**
     - Creating RESTful APIs that run on AWS Lambda.
     - Using Flask or FastAPI to handle HTTP requests and trigger Lambda functions.

9. **Pytest for Unit Testing**

   Pytest is a testing framework that makes it easy to write simple and scalable test cases for your Python code. Writing unit tests for serverless functions is important to ensure that your application behaves as expected. With Pytest, you can write tests for your Python-based Lambda functions and integrate them into your continuous integration (CI) pipeline.

- **Example Use Cases:**
  - Writing unit tests for Lambda functions.
  - Testing interactions with AWS services (e.g., DynamoDB, S3) locally using mocking libraries like **moto**.

10. **Moto for Mocking AWS Services**

Moto is a Python library that allows you to mock AWS services locally during testing. It is particularly useful when testing serverless applications locally, as it lets you simulate interactions with AWS services like S3, DynamoDB, and Lambda without needing to interact with real AWS infrastructure. This reduces testing costs and allows you to write unit tests for serverless functions without requiring an actual AWS account.

- **Example Use Cases:**
  - Mocking AWS S3 to test file uploads without hitting the real S3 service.
  - Simulating DynamoDB interactions to test how Lambda functions perform database operations.

These libraries, combined with Python's own strengths, make it an excellent choice for building serverless applications. Whether you're working with APIs, databases, or cloud services, these libraries streamline the development process and help you build efficient, scalable, and cost-effective serverless applications.

Python Syntax Review (Brief) for Beginners

Before diving deeper into serverless development, it's important to have a basic understanding of Python syntax. If you're new to Python, don't worry—this brief review will cover the most essential syntax you need to know for serverless development.

1. **Variables and Data Types**

   In Python, you don't need to explicitly declare variable types. Python automatically assigns a type based on the value assigned to the variable. Here are some basic data types:

Strings: Text enclosed in single or double quotes.

python

Copy

```
name = "John Doe"
```

- **Integers**: Whole numbers.

  python

  Copy

  ```
  age = 30
  ```

- **Floats**: Decimal numbers.

  python

  Copy

  ```
  price = 19.99
  ```

- **Booleans**: True or False values.

  python

  Copy

  ```
  is_active = True
  ```

2. Lists and Dictionaries

Lists: Ordered collections of items.

python

Copy

fruits = ["apple", "banana", "orange"]

- **Dictionaries**: Unordered collections of key-value pairs.

  python

  Copy

  user = {"name": "Alice", "age": 25}

- **Functions**

  Functions in Python are defined using the def keyword. Functions allow you to reuse code and make your serverless functions more modular.

  python

  Copy

  def greet(name):

  return f"Hello, {name}!"

print(greet("World"))

3. Control Flow

If-Else Statements: Used for conditional execution.

python

Copy

if age >= 18:

    print("Adult")

else:

    print("Minor")

- ○ **For Loops**: Used to iterate over a collection (like a list or dictionary).

python

Copy

```
for fruit in fruits:

    print(fruit)
```

- ○ **Error Handling with Try-Except**

Python uses the try and except blocks to handle exceptions (errors). This is useful when dealing with potential errors in serverless functions, such as file access or API calls.

python

Copy

```
try:

    result = 10 / 0
except ZeroDivisionError:
    print("Cannot divide by zero!")
```

4. **Lambda Functions**

Lambda functions are small anonymous functions defined using the lambda keyword. These are useful for short, one-off functions, often used in serverless applications.

python

Copy

```
square = lambda x: x * x

print(square(5))  # Output: 25
```

5. **Asynchronous Programming**

For serverless applications, especially those interacting with external resources (like databases or APIs), asynchronous programming is important. Python's asyncio library allows you to run tasks concurrently, improving performance when dealing with I/O-bound operations.

python

Copy

```python
import asyncio


async def fetch_data():
    await asyncio.sleep(2)
    return "Data fetched"


async def main():
    data = await fetch_data()
    print(data)


asyncio.run(main())
```

Python's straightforward syntax, combined with its vast library ecosystem, makes it an excellent choice for building serverless applications. With tools like Boto3 for interacting with AWS services and frameworks like Zappa for deploying serverless apps, Python empowers developers to build and manage scalable, cost-effective applications with ease. In the next chapter, we'll set up the environment to start working with Python on AWS Lambda and explore how to deploy your first serverless function.

Chapter 3: Setting Up Your Environment

In this chapter, we will guide you through the essential steps required to set up your development environment for building serverless applications using Python. You'll need to install Python, configure the AWS Command Line Interface (CLI), and set up an AWS Free Tier account to start using AWS Lambda and other cloud services. Once you have your environment ready, we'll also introduce you to the AWS Management Console, where you can manage your serverless resources.

Installing Python and AWS CLI

Before you can start building serverless applications with Python, you need to have Python and the AWS CLI installed and configured. Let's walk through the installation process.

1. **Installing Python**

   Python is the core programming language we'll be using for building serverless applications. If Python isn't already installed on your system, follow these steps:
   - **Windows:**
     - Visit the official Python website: python.org.
     - Download the latest version of Python for Windows (usually the recommended version).
     - During installation, **check the box that says "Add Python to PATH"**. This will make Python accessible from the command line.

After installation, open a command prompt and type:
bash

Copy

python --version

- This command should output the version of Python you installed, confirming that the installation was successful.
  - **MacOS/Linux:** Python typically comes pre-installed on MacOS and most Linux distributions. However, if you need to install or upgrade Python:

Open a terminal and type:

bash

Copy

python3 --version

- If Python is not installed or you need a newer version, run the following commands:

MacOS (using Homebrew):

bash

Copy

brew install python

Linux (using apt for Ubuntu/Debian-based systems):

bash

Copy

sudo apt-get install python3

2. **Installing the AWS CLI**

The AWS CLI is a command-line tool that enables you to interact with AWS services, including AWS Lambda, directly from your terminal. Let's install it:

- **Windows:**
  - Visit the AWS CLI installation page: AWS CLI Installation.
  - Download the installer for Windows and run the setup.

Once the installation is complete, open a new Command Prompt window and type:

bash

Copy

aws --version

- This should display the version of the AWS CLI you installed.
  - ○ **MacOS/Linux:**
    - Open a terminal and run the following command to install the AWS CLI (using Homebrew on MacOS or apt on Linux):

MacOS:

bash

Copy

brew install awscli

Linux:

bash

Copy

sudo apt-get install awscli

- After installation, check if it's installed correctly by typing:
  bash
  Copy
  aws --version

3. Now that you have the AWS CLI installed, you need to configure it with your AWS account credentials.

4. **Configuring the AWS CLI**

   To configure the AWS CLI, you need to set your **Access Key ID**, **Secret Access Key**, and **region**. If you don't have an AWS account, you'll need to create one (see the next section).

Open a terminal or command prompt and run:

bash

Copy

aws configure

- You will be prompted to enter your:
  - **AWS Access Key ID**: This is provided when you create an IAM user in AWS (discussed below).
  - **AWS Secret Access Key**: Also provided along with the Access Key ID.
  - **Default region name**: Enter the region closest to you, such as us-east-1 (North Virginia).
  - **Default output format**: You can choose between json, yaml, or text. The default is typically json.
5. This will set up your AWS CLI configuration so you can begin interacting with AWS services directly from the terminal.

Setting Up AWS Free Tier Account

If you haven't already, you'll need to create an **AWS account** in order to use AWS Lambda and other AWS services. AWS provides a **Free Tier** that allows you to use many services for free within certain limits.

1. **Creating an AWS Account**
   - Go to the AWS homepage: aws.amazon.com.
   - Click on **"Create a Free Account"** and follow the instructions.
   - You will be asked to enter your email address, password, and a name for your AWS account.
   - AWS will also require a credit card for verification, but don't worry: if you stay within the Free Tier limits, you won't be charged.

2. **AWS Free Tier Overview**

   The AWS Free Tier provides a limited amount of resources free of charge for the first 12 months after you sign up. After 12 months, you'll be charged for any services used above the Free Tier limits. Here are some of the key Free Tier services relevant to serverless development:

   - **AWS Lambda**: 1 million free requests and 400,000 GB-seconds of compute time per month.
   - **Amazon S3**: 5 GB of standard storage, 20,000 GET requests, and 2,000 PUT requests per month.
   - **Amazon DynamoDB**: 25 GB of storage, 25 write capacity units, and 25 read capacity units.
   - **API Gateway**: 1 million API calls per month.

3. By staying within these limits, you can experiment and build serverless applications without worrying about incurring costs.

Introduction to the AWS Management Console

The **AWS Management Console** is a web-based interface where you can manage all your AWS services and resources. It provides a user-friendly way to interact with AWS, making it easier to create, configure, and monitor your serverless applications.

Here's how to get started with the AWS Management Console:

1. **Accessing the AWS Management Console**
   - Visit the AWS Management Console.
   - Log in with your AWS account credentials (the ones you created during the account setup process).
2. **Navigating the Console** Once logged in, you'll see the AWS Management Console homepage. The interface is organized into various sections, each

representing a different AWS service. The most commonly used services for serverless development include:

- o **AWS Lambda**: Where you can create, configure, and manage your Lambda functions.
- o **API Gateway**: To manage RESTful APIs and link them with Lambda functions.
- o **DynamoDB**: To create and manage your serverless NoSQL database.
- o **S3**: To manage file storage for your serverless applications.

3. The top bar in the console also includes a search bar that you can use to quickly navigate to any service.

4. **Creating a Lambda Function** To create your first Lambda function:

- o From the AWS Management Console, click on **Lambda** under "Services."
- o Click on **Create function**.
- o Choose **Author from scratch** and give your function a name.
- o Select **Python 3.x** as the runtime (since we're using Python for serverless development).
- o Choose an existing role or create a new role with basic Lambda permissions. (You'll learn about IAM roles in later chapters.)
- o Click **Create function**, and your function will be ready to use.

5. **Deploying and Monitoring Lambda Functions**

- o After you create your Lambda function, you can edit your code directly in the console or upload it via a ZIP file or from S3.
- o You can configure triggers for your Lambda function, such as API Gateway, DynamoDB Streams, or S3 events, directly from the Lambda console page.
- o The console also provides useful metrics and logs for monitoring function performance. You can view the execution logs via **CloudWatch Logs**.

With Python and the AWS CLI set up, an AWS Free Tier account in place, and the AWS Management Console introduced, you are now ready to dive into building your first serverless application using AWS Lambda. These steps provide the foundation for working in the AWS cloud, and next, we'll walk through writing and deploying your first Python-based Lambda function.

Creating Your First AWS Lambda Function

Now that you've set up your environment, it's time to start building your first AWS Lambda function using Python. This section will guide you through creating a basic Lambda function, configuring triggers, and testing it to ensure it works properly. We'll also walk through the process of assigning permissions using IAM roles, which are essential for ensuring your Lambda function has access to the necessary resources.

Creating Your First AWS Lambda Function

To get started, let's create a simple Python-based Lambda function that responds to an event, such as an HTTP request or a file being uploaded to S3. We'll break down the process into the following steps:

1. **Accessing AWS Lambda in the Management Console**
   - First, log into your AWS Management Console.
   - In the search bar, type **Lambda** and select it from the list of services.
   - This will bring you to the AWS Lambda dashboard where you can create and manage your Lambda functions.
2. **Creating the Lambda Function**
   - On the Lambda dashboard, click the **Create function** button.

- ○ Choose **Author from scratch**, which will allow us to define the function's settings manually.
- ○ You'll be prompted to configure the following settings:
  - **Function Name**: Give your function a unique name, such as hello_world_lambda.
  - **Runtime**: Select **Python 3.x** from the dropdown menu. This ensures the Lambda function will run using the Python runtime.
  - **Role**: Under the **Permissions** section, choose **Create a new role with basic Lambda permissions**. This will automatically create a new IAM role for your Lambda function that grants it basic execution permissions.

3. Once you've filled in the necessary information, click **Create function**. AWS will create the function and bring you to the function's management page, where you can edit the code, configure triggers, and monitor its execution.

Writing the Lambda Function Code

On the function's management page, you'll see an inline code editor where you can write your Python code. For your first function, let's create a simple Python script that responds to an event.

In the editor, paste the following Python code:

python

Copy

```python
def lambda_handler(event, context):
    # The event object contains information about the triggering event
    return {
        'statusCode': 200,
        'body': 'Hello, world!'
    }
```

4. This is a simple Lambda function that returns a message ('Hello, world!') when it is triggered. The lambda_handler function is the entry point for your Lambda function, and it accepts two arguments:
    - **event**: Contains information about the event that triggered the function (e.g., HTTP request, S3 file upload).
    - **context**: Contains metadata about the function's execution environment, such as the remaining execution time.
5. After adding the code, click **Deploy** to save your changes.
6. **Testing the Lambda Function**

    Now that your function is created, it's time to test it. AWS Lambda provides a simple way to test your function using a **test event**.
    - On the function's management page, click the **Test** button at the top of the screen.
    - You'll be prompted to configure a test event. You can select a pre-configured event template or create your own. For this simple example, select **Hello World** from the list.
    - Click **Create** to generate the test event.

Once the test event is created, click the **Test** button again to invoke the Lambda function. The results of the test will be displayed in the **Execution result** section. You should see the following output:

json

Copy

```
{
  "statusCode": 200,
  "body": "Hello, world!"
}
```

7. This confirms that your first Lambda function is working as expected. You can now explore additional features like setting up triggers and integrating your function with other AWS services.

Configuring IAM Roles for AWS Lambda

In AWS, **IAM (Identity and Access Management)** roles are used to grant permissions to your Lambda functions, allowing them to access other AWS resources such as DynamoDB, S3, or CloudWatch. When creating your Lambda function, you automatically create an IAM role with basic execution permissions. However, in most real-world applications, your function will need to access other services, so you must customize the role to include specific permissions.

Here's how to configure IAM roles for your Lambda function:

1. **Accessing IAM Roles**
   - From the AWS Management Console, search for **IAM** in the search bar and select **IAM** from the list of services.
   - In the left sidebar, click on **Roles** to view the list of IAM roles in your account.
   - Search for the role that was created for your Lambda function (e.g., lambda-role), and click on its name to view its permissions.

2. **Adding Permissions to the Role**
   In the IAM role details page, you can modify the permissions to grant your Lambda function access to other AWS services.
   - To add permissions, click the **Attach policies** button.
   - Search for the AWS service you want to grant access to. For example, if you want your Lambda function to access S3, search for **AmazonS3FullAccess**.
   - Select the policy and click **Attach policy**.

3. Now your Lambda function has the permissions to interact with S3. You can add more permissions depending on the services your function needs to access, such as DynamoDB or SNS.

41

4. **Updating Lambda Function to Use the IAM Role**

   Once you've modified the IAM role to include the necessary permissions, your Lambda function will automatically have access to the newly granted permissions. You can also modify the role assigned to a Lambda function if you need to change permissions at any time.

Connecting Python to AWS Lambda via AWS SDK (Boto3)

The **Boto3** library is the AWS SDK for Python, allowing you to interact with AWS services programmatically from your Python code. It's essential for integrating AWS resources into your serverless applications. Boto3 simplifies the process of calling AWS services, such as invoking Lambda functions, managing S3 objects, and querying DynamoDB tables.

Here's how you can connect Python to AWS Lambda via Boto3:

Installing Boto3

To use Boto3, you first need to install it. Open your terminal or command prompt and run the following command:

bash

Copy

```
pip install boto3
```

1. **Setting Up AWS Credentials**

   Before you can use Boto3 to interact with AWS services, you must configure your AWS credentials. If you haven't already done so, run the following command to configure your AWS CLI:

   bash

   Copy

   ```
   aws configure
   ```

2. Enter your AWS Access Key ID, Secret Access Key, and default region as prompted. These credentials are used by Boto3 to authenticate your requests.

Using Boto3 to Invoke a Lambda Function

With Boto3 installed and your credentials configured, you can start using Python to interact with AWS services. Let's create a Python script that invokes a Lambda function.

python

Copy

```python
import boto3

# Create a Lambda client
lambda_client = boto3.client('lambda')

# Define the Lambda function name and the event data
function_name = 'hello_world_lambda'  # Name of your Lambda function
event_data = {}  # Event data can be customized

# Invoke the Lambda function
response = lambda_client.invoke(
    FunctionName=function_name,
    InvocationType='RequestResponse',  # Wait for the response
    Payload=str(event_data)
)

# Read and print the response
response_payload = response['Payload'].read().decode('utf-8')
print(response_payload)
```

3. This script uses the boto3.client() function to create a Lambda client, then invokes the hello_world_lambda function. The invoke() method sends the event

data to the Lambda function and waits for the response. The result is printed out for you to see.

4. **Handling Lambda Function Results**

The response from the Lambda function is stored in the response_payload variable. You can process this response depending on your application's needs. For example, you can parse the JSON response or perform additional actions based on the result.

In this chapter, you've learned how to create your first AWS Lambda function with Python, configure IAM roles to manage permissions, and connect to AWS Lambda using the Boto3 SDK. You now have a functional serverless environment where you can begin experimenting with more advanced serverless workflows, such as integrating Lambda with other AWS services like S3, DynamoDB, and API Gateway.

In the next chapter, we'll dive deeper into **event-driven architectures**, where we'll explore how to trigger Lambda functions with different AWS events, including HTTP requests from API Gateway and changes in S3 buckets. This will allow you to build more interactive and powerful serverless applications.

Chapter 4: Deep Dive into AWS Lambda

AWS Lambda is one of the most widely used serverless computing services, offering a simple, yet powerful way to run code in response to various events. In this chapter, we'll take a deep dive into AWS Lambda, exploring its architecture and key features. We'll also guide you through the process of creating, deploying, and managing Lambda functions, and show you how to leverage the event-driven model to build scalable and efficient serverless applications.

Understanding AWS Lambda: Architecture and Features

AWS Lambda allows you to run code without having to provision or manage servers. It abstracts the underlying infrastructure, enabling developers to focus purely on writing the business logic. Lambda functions can be triggered by various AWS services and HTTP requests, providing the flexibility to build highly scalable, event-driven applications.

Core Components of AWS Lambda

Lambda Function

A Lambda function is a small, stateless unit of code that you write to perform specific tasks. Lambda functions are written in various languages, including Python, Node.js, Java, and more. Each function is associated with a specific runtime, and it runs in response to a defined event.

When you create a Lambda function, you can specify its **handler**, which is the entry point for the function. In Python, this is typically a Python function defined in your code that takes two parameters: event and context.

Example:

python

Copy

```
def lambda_handler(event, context):
    return {
        'statusCode': 200,
        'body': 'Hello, Lambda!'
    }
```

1. The handler defines the behavior of the Lambda function when it's invoked.
2. **Execution Role (IAM Role)**

   Lambda functions require an **IAM role** to grant them permissions to interact with other AWS resources. This role defines what services the Lambda function can access, such as S3 buckets, DynamoDB tables, or SQS queues. When creating a Lambda function, you either specify an existing IAM role or create a new one with the required permissions.
3. **Event Sources**

   AWS Lambda functions are triggered by events, which are sent by other AWS services or external sources. Common event sources include:
   - **API Gateway** for HTTP requests.
   - **S3** for file uploads.
   - **DynamoDB** for database changes.
   - **SQS** or **SNS** for messaging events.
4. The event source sends data to the Lambda function, which processes it and returns a response or performs an action based on the event.
5. **Event Payload**

   When a Lambda function is triggered, it receives an **event** object that contains data relevant to the event source. For example, an S3 event might include details about the file uploaded, while an API Gateway event might include HTTP request data. The event object is passed to the function handler as the first parameter, and the function processes it according to the logic you define.

46

6. **Lambda Function Configuration**

When you create a Lambda function, you configure several settings:

- ○ **Memory Allocation**: Defines how much memory the function is allocated, which impacts the CPU and performance.
- ○ **Timeout**: Specifies how long the function is allowed to run before AWS stops it. This is typically set based on the expected duration of the function.
- ○ **Environment Variables**: Key-value pairs that can be used to pass configuration settings to the Lambda function at runtime.

Lambda Pricing Model

Lambda's pricing is based on the number of **requests** and the **compute time** your function consumes. The cost is calculated as:

- **Requests**: You are charged per 1 million requests.
- **Duration**: You are charged based on the amount of memory allocated to the function and the duration the function runs (measured in milliseconds).

The pricing is highly cost-effective, especially for workloads that have unpredictable or intermittent traffic, since you only pay when your functions are invoked.

Creating and Deploying Your First Lambda Function

Now that you understand the basics of AWS Lambda's architecture, let's walk through the process of creating and deploying a Lambda function step by step.

Step 1: Create the Lambda Function

1. **Access AWS Lambda**

   Log in to your AWS Management Console and navigate to **Lambda** by searching for it in the services search bar.

2. **Create a New Lambda Function**

   Click **Create function**, and you'll be prompted to configure your Lambda function. Select the following options:
   - **Function Name**: first_lambda_function
   - **Runtime**: Select **Python 3.x.**
   - **Role**: Select **Create a new role with basic Lambda permissions**. This creates a role with permissions to execute the Lambda function.

Write Your Code

In the **Function code** section, you'll see an inline editor. Replace the default code with the following Python function:

python

Copy

```
def lambda_handler(event, context):
    return {
        'statusCode': 200,
        'body': 'Hello, Lambda World!'
    }
```

3. This function simply returns a message indicating it was invoked.

4. **Deploy the Function**

   Once you've written the code, click **Deploy** to save your changes. AWS will package and deploy your function.

Step 2: Test Your Lambda Function

1. **Configure a Test Event**

   To test the function, click on **Test**. You'll be prompted to configure a test event, which is a simulated input that mimics what the Lambda function will receive when it's triggered.

   - Choose **Hello World** as the test event template.
   - Click **Save changes** and then **Test** to invoke the function.

View Test Results

After testing, you'll see the execution results in the **Execution result** section. You should see the output:

json

Copy

```
{
  "statusCode": 200,
  "body": "Hello, Lambda World!"
}
```

2. This confirms that your Lambda function was successfully invoked and returned the correct result.

Event-Driven Programming with AWS Lambda

The true power of AWS Lambda comes from its **event-driven architecture**. Lambda functions can be triggered by a wide range of events from other AWS services. This allows you to build applications that respond to real-time events, such as HTTP requests, file uploads, database changes, or messages from queues.

Let's explore some common event sources and how they trigger Lambda functions.

Common Event Sources

1. **API Gateway (HTTP Requests)**

   API Gateway is often used to expose Lambda functions as RESTful APIs. When a client makes an HTTP request (such as a GET or POST request), API Gateway triggers the associated Lambda function to process the request.

   Example: A simple API that responds with "Hello, World!" when accessed via a web browser or an HTTP client like Postman.

2. **Amazon S3 (File Uploads)**

   Lambda can be triggered when an object is uploaded to an S3 bucket. For example, if you're building an image processing app, you could configure Lambda to automatically resize images upon upload.

   Example: When an image is uploaded to an S3 bucket, Lambda processes the image (e.g., resizing or watermarking) and stores the modified image in another S3 bucket.

3. **Amazon DynamoDB (Table Changes)**

   Lambda functions can be triggered by changes to a DynamoDB table, such as an item being added, updated, or deleted. This is useful for building real-time applications that respond to changes in a database.

   Example: A Lambda function that sends an email notification when a new record is added to a DynamoDB table.

4. **Amazon SQS (Queue Messages)**

   AWS Lambda can process messages from an SQS queue, allowing you to build event-driven, asynchronous processing systems.

   Example: A Lambda function that processes orders from a shopping cart queue, updating inventory and triggering shipping processes.

5. **Amazon SNS (Simple Notification Service)**

   Lambda can also be triggered by messages from SNS topics. This is commonly used for pub/sub messaging systems where multiple Lambda functions may need to react to different messages from a single topic.

Example: A Lambda function that triggers an SMS notification to a user when a certain event happens, like when their order has been shipped.

Creating an Event Trigger

Let's take an example of triggering your Lambda function using **API Gateway**:

1. **Set Up API Gateway**

    In the Lambda function management page, scroll to the **Designer** section and click **Add trigger**.
    - Select **API Gateway** as the trigger.
    - Choose **Create an API** and select **REST API**.
    - Under **Security**, choose **Open** (for simplicity in this example, but in real scenarios, you'll want to configure authentication).
    - Click **Add** to create the API Gateway trigger.

2. **Test the API**

    After creating the API, AWS will automatically generate a URL for you. You can use this URL to test your Lambda function by making HTTP requests.

    You can use tools like **Postman** or **curl** to make GET or POST requests to the URL. The Lambda function will respond with the same "Hello, Lambda World!" message defined in the function code.

We've delved deeper into the architecture and features of AWS Lambda. We've created and deployed our first Lambda function and tested it to ensure it works correctly. We also explored the event-driven nature of Lambda and how it interacts with different AWS services such as API Gateway, S3, DynamoDB, and more.

With Lambda's event-driven model, you can build highly scalable, resilient, and cost-effective applications that respond to real-time events. Next chapter, we'll explore how to configure your Lambda functions to work seamlessly with various event sources, and how to optimize them for performance and scalability.

Exploring Lambda Triggers: API Gateway, DynamoDB, S3, and More

We've covered the basics of AWS Lambda, how to create and deploy a function, and how it can be triggered by various events. In this chapter, we'll dive deeper into some of the most common Lambda event triggers: **API Gateway**, **DynamoDB**, **S3**, and more. We'll also discuss **Lambda execution time**, its **limits**, and **best practices** for building efficient serverless applications.

Lambda Triggers: API Gateway, DynamoDB, S3, and More

AWS Lambda functions can be triggered by a variety of events coming from different AWS services. By integrating Lambda with other services, you can build event-driven, fully serverless applications. Let's explore the most common triggers and how they can be configured.

---

1. API Gateway (HTTP Requests)

One of the most popular ways to trigger Lambda functions is through **API Gateway**, which allows you to expose your Lambda function as a RESTful API. This setup is perfect for building serverless web applications and APIs.

How it Works: API Gateway acts as a reverse proxy to handle incoming HTTP requests (GET, POST, PUT, DELETE, etc.) and forwards those requests to your Lambda function. The function processes the request and returns the response, which API Gateway then sends back to the client.

Setting Up API Gateway:

1. Go to the AWS Lambda function you want to trigger via API Gateway.
2. Scroll down to the **Designer** section, click **Add trigger**, and select **API Gateway**.
3. Choose **Create an API**, select **REST API**, and configure the settings:
   - **Security**: Choose whether to make the API public or secure it with AWS IAM or Cognito.
   - **API Name**: Provide a name for the API.
   - **Endpoint Type**: Choose between **Regional** or **Edge-Optimized** (Edge-Optimized is better for global applications).
4. After configuring, API Gateway will automatically generate a URL, which can be used to access your Lambda function.

Example Use Case: A simple API endpoint that accepts a POST request to create a new user:

python

Copy

```python
def lambda_handler(event, context):

    # Extract the data from the event object (which is the HTTP request body)

    user_data = json.loads(event['body'])

    # Process the data (e.g., store it in DynamoDB)

    return {

        'statusCode': 201,

        'body': json.dumps('User created successfully!')
```

53

2. DynamoDB (Table Changes)

AWS Lambda can be triggered automatically by changes to a **DynamoDB** table. This is an excellent way to react to real-time updates in your database, such as when an item is added, updated, or deleted.

How it Works: When a write (PutItem, UpdateItem, or DeleteItem) occurs in DynamoDB, the change is captured by DynamoDB Streams, which triggers the Lambda function. The event passed to Lambda contains details about the change, allowing you to process the updated data.

Setting Up DynamoDB Trigger:

1. In the Lambda console, click **Add trigger** and choose **DynamoDB**.
2. Select the DynamoDB table you want to monitor.
3. Configure the **Stream view type**. Options include:
   o **NEW_IMAGE**: The full item as it appears after the update.
   o **OLD_IMAGE**: The full item as it appeared before the update.
   o **NEW_AND_OLD_IMAGES**: Both versions of the item.
4. Set the **Batch size**, which determines how many records Lambda will process in one invocation.

Example Use Case: A Lambda function that logs the changes made to a DynamoDB table:

python

Copy

```
def lambda_handler(event, context):
```

54

```python
for record in event['Records']:

    # Log the change (new or old image of the DynamoDB item)

    print(record['dynamodb'])

return 'Processed ' + str(len(event['Records'])) + ' records.'
```

---

3. Amazon S3 (File Uploads and Changes)

Another common trigger for Lambda functions is **Amazon S3**. Lambda can be configured to run when an object is uploaded, deleted, or modified in an S3 bucket.

How it Works: When an object is uploaded to an S3 bucket, the event notification triggers a Lambda function. The event payload contains information about the file, such as the bucket name and the object key, which can be used to process or manipulate the file.

Setting Up S3 Trigger:

1. Go to the S3 bucket you want to monitor.
2. Under **Properties**, scroll down to the **Event notifications** section and click **Create event notification**.
3. Set the event type (e.g., **All object create events, Delete events**).
4. Select **Lambda Function** as the destination and choose your Lambda function.

Example Use Case: A Lambda function that automatically resizes images uploaded to an S3 bucket:

python

Copy

```python
from PIL import Image
import boto3


def lambda_handler(event, context):
    s3 = boto3.client('s3')
    bucket = event['Records'][0]['s3']['bucket']['name']
    key = event['Records'][0]['s3']['object']['key']

    # Download the image from S3
    file_obj = s3.get_object(Bucket=bucket, Key=key)
    img = Image.open(file_obj['Body'])

    # Resize the image
    img = img.resize((200, 200))

    # Save the resized image back to S3
    img.save('/tmp/resized_image.jpg')
    s3.upload_file('/tmp/resized_image.jpg', bucket, 'resized_' + key)
```

56

return 'Image resized and uploaded successfully.'

---

4. Amazon SQS (Simple Queue Service)

Amazon SQS is a fully managed message queue service that can be used to decouple and scale microservices, distributed systems, and serverless applications. Lambda functions can be triggered by messages placed in an SQS queue.

How it Works: When a message is added to an SQS queue, it triggers the associated Lambda function. This is useful for applications that need to process tasks asynchronously, such as order processing, sending emails, or handling background jobs.

Setting Up SQS Trigger:

1. In the Lambda console, click **Add trigger** and select **SQS**.
2. Choose the SQS queue you want to monitor.
3. Lambda will automatically process messages from the queue. You can configure the batch size to control how many messages are processed at once.

Example Use Case: A Lambda function that processes order messages from an SQS queue:

python

Copy

```
def lambda_handler(event, context):

    for record in event['Records']:

        order = record['body']
```

```
print(f"Processing order: {order}")

return 'Processed ' + str(len(event['Records'])) + ' messages.'
```

Lambda Execution Time and Limits: Best Practices

Lambda functions have certain execution limits that are important to understand when building and deploying serverless applications. These limits ensure that Lambda functions are efficient and scalable, but they also mean you need to optimize your functions to work within these constraints.

1. Lambda Timeout Limit

Each Lambda function has a configurable timeout setting, which determines how long the function is allowed to run before AWS automatically stops it. The maximum timeout is **15 minutes** (900 seconds). If your function exceeds this time, it will be forcibly terminated.

Best Practice: Always set the timeout value to the minimum amount of time your function needs to execute. Avoid setting unnecessarily high timeouts, as this could lead to wasted resources. For long-running processes, consider breaking them up into smaller tasks or using AWS Step Functions.

2. Memory Allocation

Lambda functions allow you to allocate memory between 128 MB and 10,240 MB (10 GB). The more memory you allocate, the more CPU and networking bandwidth your function receives. However, increasing memory also increases the cost, so finding the right balance is important.

58

Best Practice: Start with a small memory allocation (e.g., 512 MB) and test your function's performance. If the function is slow or has a high execution time, gradually increase the memory allocation until you find an optimal level that balances speed and cost.

3. Concurrency Limits

Lambda functions have a concurrency limit, which is the number of instances of your function that can run simultaneously. By default, the **concurrent execution limit** for AWS accounts is set to **1,000** concurrent invocations across all functions in the account. You can request an increase in this limit if necessary.

Best Practice: For high-concurrency applications, such as APIs with high traffic, use **API Gateway** with Lambda to manage the load. You can also configure Lambda to trigger multiple instances of functions in parallel, ensuring that your application can scale as needed.

4. Payload Size Limit

Lambda functions have a payload size limit of **6 MB** for synchronous invocations (e.g., from API Gateway) and **256 KB** for asynchronous invocations (e.g., from S3 or DynamoDB). This means the event data you send to Lambda, including request data, must be within these limits.

Best Practice: If your event data exceeds the payload size limit, consider using Amazon S3 to store large files and pass S3 object references (e.g., bucket name and object key) to Lambda instead of the entire file.

5. Cold Start Latency

Cold starts occur when AWS Lambda initializes a new instance of a function to handle a request, which can result in additional latency. Cold start times can vary depending on the function's size and dependencies.

Best Practice: Minimize the dependencies in your Lambda function, as large libraries and packages can increase cold start time. Use **AWS Lambda layers** to manage external dependencies efficiently.

In this chapter, we explored some of the most commonly used Lambda triggers, including **API Gateway, DynamoDB, S3**, and **SQS,** and discussed how to configure these event sources to trigger Lambda functions. We also covered Lambda's execution limits and best practices for optimizing performance and reducing costs.

By understanding and utilizing these triggers, you can build highly scalable, efficient, and event-driven serverless applications. In the next chapter, we'll focus on optimizing Lambda performance further and integrating Lambda with other AWS services for building end-to-end serverless solutions.

Chapter 5: Building Serverless Applications with Python

In this chapter, we'll explore the process of designing and building serverless applications using Python and AWS Lambda. We'll introduce you to the **Serverless Application Model (SAM)**, a framework that simplifies the development of serverless applications. Additionally, we'll show you how to build REST APIs using **AWS API Gateway** and Python to allow your serverless apps to interact with users and external services.

Designing Serverless Apps Using AWS Lambda and Python

Building serverless applications with AWS Lambda and Python involves designing a system that responds to specific events, processes them, and interacts with other AWS services, all without managing traditional servers. Let's break down the key steps involved in designing a serverless app:

1. **Event-Driven Architecture**
   Serverless applications are often **event-driven**, meaning that a specific event triggers the execution of a Lambda function. Common event sources include:
   - **API Gateway** for HTTP requests.
   - **S3** for file uploads.
   - **DynamoDB Streams** for database changes.
   - **SQS** and **SNS** for messaging.
2. When designing serverless applications, you must determine the events that will trigger your Lambda functions. These events could originate from any of these

services or even external triggers, like an HTTP request sent from a web browser or a message placed in an SQS queue.

3. **Components of Serverless Applications**

A typical serverless application built with AWS Lambda and Python consists of the following components:

- **Lambda Functions**: These are the core of your application. Each function performs a specific task, such as processing data, interacting with a database, or calling an external API.
- **Event Sources**: These trigger your Lambda functions. For example, an API request from a user might trigger a Lambda function to return a response.
- **AWS Services Integration**: AWS services like **DynamoDB, S3**, and **SNS** can be used to store data, trigger events, or send notifications.
- **IAM Roles**: Permissions that define what AWS services your Lambda functions can interact with, ensuring proper security.

4. **Design Considerations for Serverless Apps**

When designing serverless applications, there are several important considerations:

- **Statelessness**: Lambda functions should be stateless, meaning they don't rely on the data from previous executions. If you need to store or maintain state, you can use services like DynamoDB or S3.
- **Scalability**: Serverless applications automatically scale with demand. Lambda functions will scale horizontally, meaning more instances of your function are created to handle higher traffic or load.
- **Cost Efficiency**: Serverless applications are highly cost-efficient because you only pay for the resources you actually use. Lambda's pay-per-use model means that you don't incur costs when your application is idle.
- **Event-Driven**: Design your application around events. AWS Lambda makes it easy to integrate with various AWS services, allowing your app to react to real-time events.

5. **Common Use Cases for Serverless Apps**

   Here are some common use cases for serverless applications:

   ○ **Real-Time File Processing**: When a user uploads a file to S3, a Lambda function can process the file (e.g., resize images, parse data, or convert formats).

   ○ **Web Backends**: Using API Gateway with Lambda, you can build a serverless backend for web or mobile apps that responds to user requests, such as creating, updating, or retrieving data from a database.

   ○ **Event-Driven Data Pipelines**: Serverless functions can be used to process data as it's streamed from sources like DynamoDB, SQS, or SNS, enabling real-time data processing pipelines.

Understanding Serverless Application Models (SAM)

The **Serverless Application Model (SAM)** is an open-source framework that simplifies the development and deployment of serverless applications. SAM is built on top of AWS CloudFormation, which allows you to define your serverless application resources in a declarative template. SAM simplifies the creation and management of Lambda functions, API Gateway endpoints, DynamoDB tables, and other serverless resources by providing shorthand syntax for CloudFormation.

1. **Key Components of SAM**

   ○ **AWS::Serverless::Function**: Defines an AWS Lambda function.

   ○ **AWS::Serverless::Api**: Defines an API Gateway resource for HTTP access to your Lambda functions.

   ○ **AWS::Serverless::SimpleTable**: Defines a simple DynamoDB table.

2. SAM allows you to define these resources in a template.yaml file, making it easier to create and manage serverless resources in a declarative way.

3. **SAM CLI**

   The **SAM CLI** (Command Line Interface) is a tool that makes it easier to develop, test, and deploy serverless applications. With the SAM CLI, you can:

   - **Initialize a Serverless Application**: Create a new project with sample templates.
   - **Build and Test Locally**: Simulate Lambda function execution locally and test it with different event sources before deploying.
   - **Deploy to AWS**: Deploy your application using SAM, which automates the process of creating CloudFormation stacks and managing resources.

4. You can install SAM CLI on your local machine by following the instructions in the official AWS SAM documentation.

5. **Using SAM for Serverless Application Deployment**

   The process of deploying a serverless application with SAM involves the following steps:

   - **Write the Template**: Define your Lambda function, API Gateway, and other resources in the template.yaml file.
   - **Build the Application**: Run sam build to compile and prepare the application for deployment.
   - **Deploy the Application**: Run sam deploy to create the CloudFormation stack and deploy your resources to AWS.

Example SAM Template for a Simple Lambda Function and API Gateway:

yaml

Copy

```
AWSTemplateFormatVersion: '2010-09-09'
Transform: 'AWS::Serverless-2016-10-31'

Resources:
  HelloWorldFunction:
    Type: 'AWS::Serverless::Function'
```

64

```
Properties:
  Handler: hello_world.lambda_handler
  Runtime: python3.8
  CodeUri: ./src
  MemorySize: 128
  Timeout: 5
  Events:
   Api:
    Type: Api
    Properties:
     Path: /hello
     Method: get

ApiGateway:
 Type: AWS::Serverless::Api
 Properties:
  Name: HelloWorldApi
  StageName: prod
```

6. In this example:
   - We define a Lambda function (HelloWorldFunction) that responds to GET requests at the /hello endpoint using API Gateway.
   - The CodeUri specifies the location of the Lambda function's code.
   - We also define an API Gateway resource (ApiGateway) that will trigger the Lambda function.

7. **Benefits of Using SAM**
   - **Simplified Resource Management**: SAM abstracts complex CloudFormation syntax, making it easier to manage Lambda functions, API Gateway, DynamoDB, and other serverless resources.

- o **Local Development**: SAM CLI allows for local testing and debugging of serverless functions, making it easier to test code before deploying to AWS.
- o **Consistent Environments**: SAM helps ensure that your development, staging, and production environments are consistent.

Building REST APIs with AWS API Gateway and Python

One of the most common use cases for Lambda is building a **RESTful API** that can interact with web and mobile applications. AWS API Gateway, when combined with Lambda, allows you to easily expose your Lambda functions as HTTP endpoints.

Let's walk through the steps to create a simple REST API using **API Gateway** and **Lambda**:

Creating a Lambda Function

First, we need to create a Lambda function that will handle HTTP requests. In this example, our function will return a simple greeting.

In the Lambda console, create a new function and use the following code:

python

Copy

```python
def lambda_handler(event, context):
    name = event.get('queryStringParameters', {}).get('name', 'World')
    message = f'Hello, {name}!'
    return {
        'statusCode': 200,
        'body': message
    }
```

1. This function looks for a name query parameter in the event object and returns a personalized greeting. If no name is provided, it defaults to "World."

2. **Creating an API Gateway**

   Next, create an API Gateway to expose this Lambda function as an HTTP endpoint:

   - In the Lambda function configuration, scroll down to the **Designer** section.
   - Click **Add trigger**, select **API Gateway**, and choose **Create an API**.
   - Choose **REST API** and configure the **API Name** and **Endpoint Type**.
   - For the **Security** option, you can choose **Open** for public access or configure authentication as needed.

3. **Deploying the API**

   Once the API Gateway trigger is set up, deploy the API to make it accessible:

   - In the API Gateway dashboard, click on **Actions** and select **Deploy API**.
   - Choose the deployment stage (e.g., prod).
   - After deploying, API Gateway will generate a URL for the API, which you can use to invoke the Lambda function via HTTP.

Testing the API

Use a browser or tool like **Postman** to make a GET request to the generated URL. Add a name query parameter to test the function:

bash

Copy

https://your-api-id.execute-api.us-east-1.amazonaws.com/prod/hello?name=John

The response should be:

json

Copy

"Hello, John!"

If no name parameter is provided:

json

Copy
"Hello, World!"

4.

We've explored how to design serverless applications using Python and AWS Lambda. We covered the basics of using the **Serverless Application Model (SAM)** to deploy and manage serverless resources efficiently. We also learned how to build REST APIs using **API Gateway** and **Lambda** to expose your functions as HTTP endpoints.

Serverless applications built with Python, AWS Lambda, and other AWS services like API Gateway, DynamoDB, and S3 provide a highly scalable and cost-effective way to build modern applications. Next, we'll delve into **security and access control** for your serverless applications, covering how to securely manage and protect your Lambda functions and other AWS resources.

Connecting to Databases: DynamoDB vs RDS

In this chapter, we will explore how to connect AWS Lambda functions to databases, comparing **DynamoDB** and **RDS** for different use cases. DynamoDB and RDS are two popular AWS database options, each suited for different types of serverless applications. By the end of this chapter, you'll understand when to use each and how to integrate them with your serverless functions.

We will also walk through a **hands-on example** of building a **serverless contact form** that interacts with DynamoDB to store and retrieve user submissions.

Connecting to Databases: DynamoDB vs RDS

When building serverless applications with AWS Lambda, choosing the right database is crucial. Let's dive into the differences between **DynamoDB** and **RDS** (Relational Database Service), two of the most commonly used databases with Lambda functions.

---

1. Amazon DynamoDB: A NoSQL Database

Amazon DynamoDB is a fully managed NoSQL database designed for high availability, scalability, and low-latency performance. It's best suited for applications that require fast and flexible querying on unstructured data, such as storing user profiles, product catalogs, or session information.

Key Features of DynamoDB:

- **Schema-less**: DynamoDB is a NoSQL database, meaning it doesn't require you to define a fixed schema upfront. You can store items with different attributes in the same table.
- **Scalability**: DynamoDB is designed to scale automatically with demand. It handles read and write operations seamlessly without manual intervention.
- **Performance**: DynamoDB provides low-latency access, even at massive scales. It's ideal for applications that require fast read and write operations, like gaming leaderboards or IoT devices.
- **Cost-Effective**: DynamoDB offers a pay-per-use model with no server management required. You pay for the storage and throughput you consume, making it highly cost-effective for variable workloads.

Use Cases for DynamoDB:

- Real-time applications (e.g., online gaming, mobile apps)
- User sessions and state management

- Product catalogs, inventory management
- Event-driven architectures

Connecting Lambda to DynamoDB: To connect AWS Lambda to DynamoDB, you use the **Boto3** SDK. Here's a simple example of how to interact with DynamoDB in a Lambda function:

python
Copy

```python
import boto3
from boto3.dynamodb.conditions import Key

# Create a DynamoDB client
dynamodb = boto3.resource('dynamodb')
table = dynamodb.Table('ContactFormSubmissions')

def lambda_handler(event, context):
    # Store form submission data in DynamoDB
    name = event['name']
    email = event['email']
    message = event['message']

    # Insert the submission into the table
    response = table.put_item(
        Item={
            'Email': email,
            'Name': name,
            'Message': message
        }
    )
    return {
```

```
'statusCode': 200,
'body': 'Submission successful!'
}
```

In this code:

- We use **Boto3** to connect to DynamoDB and insert a contact form submission.
- The event object contains the form data, and the data is inserted into the DynamoDB table.

---

2. Amazon RDS: A Relational Database Service

Amazon RDS is a fully managed relational database service that supports multiple engines, including MySQL, PostgreSQL, Oracle, and SQL Server. RDS is ideal for applications that require complex queries, transactional integrity, and well-defined relationships between data.

Key Features of RDS:

- **SQL Queries**: RDS supports structured query language (SQL), making it a good choice for applications that require complex queries, joins, and relationships between data.
- **ACID Transactions**: RDS supports ACID (Atomicity, Consistency, Isolation, Durability) transactions, which are important for applications that need to ensure data consistency and integrity.
- **Backup and Recovery**: RDS automatically handles backups, software patching, and failover, ensuring your data is protected and always available.
- **Scaling**: While RDS can scale vertically (by upgrading instance sizes), it doesn't scale horizontally in the same way DynamoDB does.

Use Cases for RDS:

- Applications with complex relationships and transactional data (e.g., banking apps, e-commerce platforms)
- Reporting systems that require complex joins and aggregations
- Applications that need SQL compatibility for legacy systems

Connecting Lambda to RDS: Connecting Lambda to RDS is a bit different because RDS is a relational database and usually requires establishing a persistent connection. To interact with RDS, you need to use a database driver appropriate for the database engine (e.g., **pymysql** for MySQL or **psycopg2** for PostgreSQL).

Here's a simple example using **pymysql** with MySQL in RDS:

python
Copy

```python
import pymysql
import os

# RDS configuration
rds_host = os.environ['RDS_HOST']
db_user = os.environ['DB_USER']
db_password = os.environ['DB_PASSWORD']
db_name = os.environ['DB_NAME']

def lambda_handler(event, context):
    try:
        # Connect to the RDS database
        connection = pymysql.connect(host=rds_host,
                        user=db_user,
                        password=db_password,
                        database=db_name)
```

```python
        # Insert form submission into RDS
        with connection.cursor() as cursor:
            sql = "INSERT INTO contact_form (name, email, message) VALUES (%s, %s, %s)"
            cursor.execute(sql, (event['name'], event['email'], event['message']))
            connection.commit()

        return {
            'statusCode': 200,
            'body': 'Submission successful!'
        }
    except Exception as e:
        print(f"Error: {e}")
        return {
            'statusCode': 500,
            'body': 'Failed to submit form.'
        }
```

In this example:

- We connect to an RDS instance (MySQL) using **pymysql**.
- The Lambda function inserts the form submission into a table named contact_form.

Building a Serverless Contact Form: A Hands-On Example

In this section, we'll build a simple serverless **contact form** application using AWS Lambda and **DynamoDB** as the database. The form will accept user input, store the data in DynamoDB, and send a confirmation response to the user.

Step 1: Create the DynamoDB Table

First, we need to create a DynamoDB table to store contact form submissions.

1. Go to the **DynamoDB** console in AWS.
2. Click **Create table**.
3. Define the table settings:
    - **Table name**: ContactFormSubmissions
    - **Primary key**: Email (String)
4. Click **Create** to create the table.

Step 2: Create the Lambda Function

Now, let's create a Lambda function that stores the contact form submissions in DynamoDB.

1. Go to the **Lambda** console in AWS.
2. Click **Create function** and choose **Author from scratch**.
3. Set the **Function name** to ContactFormHandler and choose **Python 3.x** as the runtime.
4. For permissions, create a new role with basic Lambda permissions.

In the **Function code** section, paste the following code:

```python
Copy
import boto3
import json
```

74

```python
# Initialize DynamoDB client
dynamodb = boto3.resource('dynamodb')
table = dynamodb.Table('ContactFormSubmissions')

def lambda_handler(event, context):
    # Extract data from the event (i.e., form submission)
    name = event['name']
    email = event['email']
    message = event['message']

    # Store the form submission in DynamoDB
    response = table.put_item(
        Item={
            'Email': email,
            'Name': name,
            'Message': message
        }
    )

    return {
        'statusCode': 200,
        'body': json.dumps('Submission successful!')
    }
```

5.

Step 3: Set Up API Gateway

Next, set up an **API Gateway** to expose the Lambda function as an HTTP endpoint.

1. In the Lambda function's designer, click **Add trigger** and select **API Gateway**.

2. Choose **Create an API** and select **REST API**.

3. Set the **API name** to ContactFormAPI.

4. Choose **Open** for security (you can configure authentication later if needed).

5. Click **Add**.

API Gateway will automatically generate a URL that can be used to trigger the Lambda function.

Step 4: Test the Contact Form

To test the contact form, you can use **Postman** or any HTTP client to send a POST request to the API Gateway URL. Include the form data in the request body, like so:

json

Copy

```
{
    "name": "John Doe",
    "email": "john.doe@example.com",
    "message": "Hello, I'd like to get in touch."
}
```

If everything is set up correctly, the Lambda function will store the submission in DynamoDB and return a confirmation message.

In this chapter, we explored how to connect AWS Lambda to two popular database options: **DynamoDB** and **RDS**. We discussed the advantages of each database type and walked through examples of how to connect Lambda functions to both DynamoDB (a NoSQL database) and RDS (a relational database). We also built a simple **serverless contact form** that stores user submissions in DynamoDB, using Lambda and API Gateway to handle the backend processing.

In the next chapter, we'll explore **security and best practices** for securing Lambda functions and the data they interact with, including how to properly configure IAM roles and policies.

Chapter 6: Cost Management and Optimization in Serverless Architecture

Serverless computing, particularly AWS Lambda, offers a highly cost-effective model for running applications because you only pay for the actual compute time and resources your function uses. However, managing and optimizing costs in a serverless architecture is essential to prevent overspending, especially as your application scales. In this chapter, we will take a deep dive into **AWS Lambda pricing and billing**, as well as explore **cost optimization strategies** to help you manage and reduce costs while ensuring optimal performance.

Understanding AWS Lambda Pricing and Billing

AWS Lambda's pricing is based on **three main factors**:

1. **Requests**
2. **Compute Time (Duration)**
3. **Memory Allocation**

Let's break down how each of these elements impacts your Lambda pricing.

1. Requests

AWS Lambda charges you based on the number of **requests** your function handles. A request is counted each time your Lambda function is invoked, whether it's triggered by an API call, an S3 file upload, or any other event.

- **Pricing**: The first 1 million requests per month are free. After that, you are charged a small fee for every million requests.

  Example:
    - **First 1 million requests**: Free
    - **Subsequent 1 million requests**: $0.20 per million requests

2. Compute Time (Duration)

The **duration** refers to the amount of time your function takes to execute. AWS Lambda charges you for every 1 millisecond your code runs, from the time your function starts executing until it returns or times out.

- **Pricing**: You are charged based on the **duration** of your function's execution, measured in 100-millisecond increments.
- **Free Tier**: The first 400,000 GB-seconds per month are free.

Billing: AWS Lambda charges for the time your function runs, multiplied by the memory allocated.

Formula:

ini

Copy

Price = (Duration in seconds) * (Memory allocated) * (Price per GB-second)

- For example, if your function runs for 1 second and you allocate 128 MB of memory, it will be billed as:
    - Duration: 1 second
    - Memory: 128 MB = 0.125 GB
    - Compute cost = 1 second * 0.125 GB * $0.00001667 per GB-second = $0.00000208

3. Memory Allocation

AWS Lambda allows you to allocate **memory** from 128 MB to 10,240 MB (10 GB). The amount of memory you allocate directly impacts both the **performance** of the function (more memory equals more CPU power) and the **cost** (more memory increases the cost).

- **Pricing**: You are charged based on the memory you allocate to your Lambda function. The more memory you allocate, the more CPU and other resources you are given. However, more memory means a higher cost.

4. Additional Costs

- **Data Transfer**: If your Lambda function communicates with other AWS services or the internet, you may incur additional costs for data transfer.
- **AWS X-Ray**: If you use AWS X-Ray for monitoring and debugging, there are additional costs for tracing Lambda invocations.
- **Provisioned Concurrency**: If you use **provisioned concurrency** (to keep certain instances of your function pre-warmed), you'll incur an additional charge for the amount of provisioned capacity.

Cost Optimization Strategies: Function Duration, Memory, and Requests

Although AWS Lambda's pricing model is already highly cost-effective, there are several strategies you can implement to optimize your costs further. These strategies focus on the three primary billing factors: function duration, memory allocation, and request volume.

---

1. Optimize Function Duration

The longer your function runs, the higher your cost will be. Optimizing the **duration** of your Lambda function is key to reducing costs. Here are some ways to minimize function execution time:

- **Efficient Code**: Write efficient code that performs tasks with minimal processing time. This means reducing the amount of time spent on looping, unnecessary calculations, and inefficient algorithms.
- **Use of Caching**: For functions that perform the same calculations or access the same data repeatedly, implement **caching** to reduce redundant calls to external services or databases. For example, you can use **Amazon CloudFront** to cache frequently requested data and reduce the load on your Lambda function.
- **Avoid Unnecessary Dependencies**: Ensure that your function includes only the libraries and dependencies that are essential for its operation. Larger code packages can slow down the cold start time and increase the duration.
- **Event Batching**: If your Lambda function processes events from a queue (e.g., **SQS**), consider **batching** multiple events into a single function invocation to reduce the overhead of invoking multiple functions.
- **Asynchronous Processing**: For tasks that don't need to be completed immediately (e.g., sending emails, background processing), consider using asynchronous invocations or offloading tasks to other services like **AWS Step Functions** or **SNS**.

---

2. Optimize Memory Allocation

Memory allocation directly impacts both performance and cost. Allocating too much memory may result in overpaying, while allocating too little may lead to slow performance or timeouts. Here's how to optimize memory allocation:

- **Benchmarking**: AWS Lambda provides a free tier for the first 400,000 GB-seconds of compute time per month. Use **AWS CloudWatch Logs** to monitor how much memory your Lambda function uses on average. If your function is consistently using only a fraction of the allocated memory, you can reduce the allocation to save costs.

- **Test Different Memory Settings**: Start with a low memory allocation and gradually increase it to see how it affects performance and cost. You can use AWS's **AWS Lambda Power Tuning** tool to run tests and find the optimal memory setting for your Lambda function.

- **Optimize Cold Start Time**: Larger memory allocations can help reduce cold start times (the time it takes for the Lambda function to initialize before processing a request). If cold start time is a bottleneck for your function, try increasing memory to improve performance.

---

3. Optimize Request Volume

The number of requests your Lambda function handles is another key cost factor. While you pay per million requests, reducing the number of unnecessary invocations can help optimize costs. Here's how to reduce request volume:

- **Event Filtering**: Set up **event filtering** to only trigger Lambda functions for specific types of events. For example, if you're processing data from an S3 bucket, you can filter events to only trigger the Lambda function for certain file types (e.g., only .jpg files).

- **Efficient Use of Triggers**: Ensure that you're only using Lambda when necessary. For example, if your Lambda function is triggered by an API Gateway, ensure that the function's code is highly efficient and handles requests quickly to avoid unnecessary invocations.

- **Combine Multiple Requests**: If your Lambda function is handling a series of similar tasks, consider batching requests together to reduce the overall number of invocations. This works particularly well with services like **SQS**, where multiple messages can be processed in a single Lambda invocation.

- **API Gateway Throttling**: If you're building a serverless API with Lambda and API Gateway, configure **API Gateway throttling** to control the rate at which requests are processed. This ensures that Lambda functions are not overwhelmed with too many requests at once, helping to control the overall cost.

---

4. Use AWS Lambda Provisioned Concurrency

Provisioned concurrency allows you to keep a set number of Lambda function instances pre-warmed and ready to handle requests immediately. While this feature can increase costs, it can also reduce cold start times for latency-sensitive applications.

When to Use Provisioned Concurrency:

- For applications where **low latency** is a critical factor (e.g., real-time user-facing applications).
- When you expect consistent traffic and want to ensure that Lambda functions are ready to handle requests immediately, reducing the startup time.

Cost Consideration: While provisioned concurrency can reduce latency, it comes with a cost. You pay for the amount of provisioned capacity, whether or not the function is invoked.

---

5. Monitor and Analyze Lambda Costs

AWS provides several tools to help you monitor and control Lambda costs:

- **AWS Cost Explorer**: Use this tool to track and analyze your Lambda costs over time. You can filter by specific Lambda functions, request volume, and other parameters to understand where your costs are coming from.
- **AWS CloudWatch Metrics**: Use CloudWatch to monitor the performance and resource usage of your Lambda functions. By reviewing metrics like **invocations**, **duration**, and **memory usage**, you can identify areas for optimization.
- **AWS Budgets**: Set up **AWS Budgets** to monitor Lambda usage and costs and receive notifications when your spending exceeds certain thresholds.

We explored AWS Lambda pricing, focusing on the key billing factors: **requests**, **compute time (duration)**, and **memory allocation**. We also discussed cost optimization strategies to help you minimize Lambda costs while maintaining the performance of your serverless applications.

By optimizing function duration, memory allocation, and request volume, you can effectively manage and reduce costs. Additionally, tools like **AWS Lambda Power Tuning**, **Provisioned Concurrency**, and **CloudWatch Metrics** can help you fine-tune your Lambda functions for both cost and performance optimization.

Minimizing Latency and Maximizing Efficiency

While AWS Lambda automatically scales with demand, there are several ways to enhance the performance of your serverless functions, ensuring they meet the latency requirements of your applications while remaining cost-effective. Additionally, we'll discuss how to use **CloudWatch** for monitoring Lambda costs and share best practices for staying within **AWS Free Tier** limits.

Minimizing Latency and Maximizing Efficiency

Lambda functions are designed to run with minimal setup and without managing servers, but optimizing for low latency and high efficiency is key to building performant serverless applications. By following certain strategies, you can reduce cold start times, optimize execution speed, and reduce the overall cost of running Lambda functions.

---

1. Reducing Cold Start Latency

Cold starts happen when AWS Lambda initializes a new instance of a function to handle a request. This initialization process can introduce latency, especially for functions with heavy dependencies or large packages.

Here are some ways to reduce cold start latency:

- **Keep Functions Lightweight**: Minimize the size of your Lambda function's deployment package by only including the libraries and dependencies that are strictly necessary. Avoid bundling large packages or dependencies that you don't need for the specific function. This reduces the time it takes for Lambda to load and initialize the function during cold starts.
- **Use Lambda Layers**: Lambda Layers are a way to manage common dependencies that are shared across multiple Lambda functions. Instead of packaging dependencies in every function, you can create a layer that contains the libraries and reference it in your functions. This reduces the function size, making cold starts faster.
- **Reduce the Initialization Time**: If your Lambda function needs to initialize resources (e.g., database connections, API clients), try to perform initialization outside the handler, so it happens only once during the first invocation. This way, subsequent invocations can benefit from the pre-initialized resources.

- **Optimize Memory Allocation**: Increasing the memory allocation for a Lambda function can reduce cold start latency by providing more CPU resources. Lambda functions with more memory are allocated more CPU power, which can speed up initialization times. However, be sure to test with different memory configurations to find the optimal balance between performance and cost.

- **Provisioned Concurrency**: If your application requires low-latency response times, consider using **Provisioned Concurrency** to keep a set number of function instances pre-warmed and ready to handle requests. This ensures that functions are always available without the need for cold starts, reducing the latency of your application. However, it comes at an additional cost, so use it judiciously.

---

2. Maximizing Function Efficiency

Maximizing the efficiency of your Lambda functions ensures that your code runs as quickly as possible, helping you reduce costs and improve performance.

Use Asynchronous Programming: For functions that involve I/O-bound operations (e.g., database queries, HTTP requests), using asynchronous programming can significantly improve efficiency. In Python, you can use asyncio or the async/await syntax to run multiple tasks concurrently without blocking the main thread. This allows Lambda to handle more requests in less time.

Example using asyncio:

python

Copy

```
import asyncio

async def fetch_data_from_db():

    # Simulate a database query
```

```python
    await asyncio.sleep(1)

    return "Data fetched"


def lambda_handler(event, context):

    data = asyncio.run(fetch_data_from_db())

    return {

        'statusCode': 200,

        'body': data

    }
```

-
- **Optimize Algorithm Efficiency**: Review your algorithms for efficiency. Avoid excessive loops or complex data structures that require a lot of computation time. If your function handles large datasets, consider optimizing your code with more efficient algorithms or using batch processing to reduce the total number of invocations.
- **Use Parallelism and Batching**: When dealing with large numbers of events, consider **batching** multiple events into a single Lambda invocation. This reduces the overhead of invoking multiple functions for individual events. Similarly, when processing large datasets, use **parallelism** to handle chunks of data simultaneously, making your Lambda function more efficient.

Using CloudWatch for Monitoring Lambda Costs

AWS **CloudWatch** provides detailed metrics, logs, and alarms to help monitor the performance and cost of your Lambda functions. By using CloudWatch effectively, you can identify areas for optimization and ensure that you stay within budget while maintaining good performance.

---

1. CloudWatch Metrics

Lambda automatically generates metrics in CloudWatch, which are available in the **CloudWatch console**. Key metrics to monitor include:

- **Invocations**: The number of times your Lambda function is called. Monitoring this metric helps you understand the volume of requests and assess whether you are hitting the Free Tier limits or exceeding expected usage.

- **Duration**: The amount of time your Lambda function takes to execute. This is important for identifying functions that take too long to run, which could lead to higher costs.

- **Errors**: The number of invocations that result in errors. A high error rate can indicate issues with your code or the resources your function depends on.

- **Throttles**: The number of times Lambda function invocations are throttled because the concurrency limit was reached. If throttling is occurring, you may need to increase your concurrency limit or optimize your functions for faster execution.

- **IteratorAge**: For functions that read from stream-based event sources (like DynamoDB Streams or Kinesis), this metric indicates the age of the last record processed. High iterator ages can suggest a backlog of events, potentially leading to delays.

---

2. CloudWatch Logs

CloudWatch Logs help you understand the execution of your Lambda function by providing detailed logs for each invocation. You can use these logs to troubleshoot errors, monitor execution time, and optimize performance.

- **Log Group and Log Streams**: Lambda automatically creates a log group for each function, and within that group, each invocation generates a log stream. You can filter and analyze the logs to identify performance bottlenecks, errors, or areas where your Lambda function is spending too much time.
- **Log Retention**: By default, CloudWatch retains logs indefinitely. However, you can configure **log retention settings** to delete logs after a specific period, helping you manage costs associated with log storage.
- **Custom Metrics**: You can also create **custom CloudWatch metrics** based on the log data to track specific application events or performance indicators.

---

3. CloudWatch Alarms

CloudWatch Alarms help you proactively monitor Lambda function behavior and costs. You can set up alarms to alert you when certain thresholds are exceeded (e.g., when the invocation count exceeds a certain limit or when duration exceeds a specified time).

- **Set Alarms for Cost Monitoring**: You can set alarms based on metrics such as **Duration, Invocations**, and **Errors** to help monitor and control costs. For example, you could set an alarm to notify you if your Lambda function execution time exceeds a certain threshold, allowing you to investigate and optimize before it leads to higher costs.

Best Practices for Staying Within Free Tier Limits

AWS offers a **Free Tier** for Lambda, providing a generous amount of free requests and compute time each month. However, staying within the Free Tier limits requires careful monitoring and optimization. Here are some best practices to help you stay within the Free Tier and avoid unexpected charges:

1. **Optimize Function Duration**: Since Lambda is billed based on execution time, reducing the duration of your function is one of the most effective ways to save costs. Make your code efficient, minimize dependencies, and reduce unnecessary operations to ensure your function runs quickly.

2. **Optimize Memory Allocation**: Start with a lower memory allocation (e.g., 128 MB) and gradually increase it if necessary. Monitoring CloudWatch metrics for **Duration** and **Memory Usage** will help you adjust memory allocation based on actual usage.

3. **Use Event Filtering**: If your Lambda function is triggered by events from services like **S3** or **SNS**, use **event filtering** to only process the relevant events. This reduces the number of unnecessary invocations and helps you stay within your Free Tier request limit.

4. **Monitor Lambda Usage**: Regularly review your Lambda usage in **AWS Cost Explorer** and **CloudWatch** to keep an eye on how many requests your Lambda functions are receiving and how much compute time they are consuming.

5. **Leverage AWS Free Tier for Development**: During development, take advantage of the **Free Tier limits** by testing your Lambda functions with low traffic and optimizing them before deploying them in a production environment.

6. **Use Lambda Reserved Concurrency**: If you have predictable traffic, use **reserved concurrency** to allocate a set amount of capacity to your functions. This ensures that you don't exceed concurrency limits, helping you maintain better control over usage and costs.

In this chapter, we covered strategies for minimizing latency and maximizing efficiency in AWS Lambda. By optimizing function duration, memory allocation, and leveraging techniques like asynchronous processing and event filtering, you can significantly improve the performance and cost-effectiveness of your serverless applications.

We also explored how to use **CloudWatch** for monitoring Lambda costs, setting alarms, and analyzing function performance to ensure your applications stay efficient. Finally, we discussed **best practices** for staying within **AWS Free Tier limits**, ensuring that you can continue to build serverless applications at minimal cost while keeping track of your usage.

In the next chapter, we'll dive into the **security** aspects of serverless applications, exploring how to secure Lambda functions, manage permissions, and protect sensitive data within your serverless environment.

Chapter 7: Security in Serverless Applications

Security is a critical consideration when building serverless applications. While serverless computing abstracts away much of the underlying infrastructure, you still need to implement proper security measures to ensure that your applications are protected from unauthorized access, data breaches, and other security threats. In this chapter, we will explore how to secure AWS Lambda functions, manage API Gateway security, and protect sensitive data using environment variables.

Securing AWS Lambda Functions: IAM Policies and Roles

AWS Lambda functions interact with various AWS resources, such as DynamoDB, S3, and SNS. To ensure your Lambda function only has the necessary permissions and does not have excessive access to resources, you need to use **IAM roles and policies**. **Identity and Access Management (IAM)** allows you to define who can access what resources, ensuring your Lambda function operates securely within the AWS ecosystem.

1. Understanding IAM Roles for Lambda

An **IAM role** is a set of permissions that define what actions a Lambda function can perform and which resources it can access. When creating a Lambda function, you must associate it with an IAM role, which dictates what the function is allowed to do.

- **IAM Role for Lambda Execution**: This role gives the Lambda function the necessary permissions to interact with other AWS resources. For example, if your Lambda function needs to access an S3 bucket, you would attach an IAM policy to the role that grants the s3:GetObject permission.

- **Best Practices for Creating IAM Roles**:
    - ○ **Principle of Least Privilege**: Always grant the least privilege necessary for your Lambda function to perform its job. Avoid using overly permissive policies like AdministratorAccess unless absolutely necessary.
    - ○ **Role Permissions for Specific AWS Services**: For example, if your Lambda function only interacts with S3, attach an S3-specific IAM policy that limits the Lambda's actions to only those required for the function.

Example IAM role policy for S3 access:

json

Copy

```json
{
  "Version": "2012-10-17",
  "Statement": [
    {
      "Effect": "Allow",
      "Action": [
        "s3:GetObject",
        "s3:PutObject"
      ],
      "Resource": "arn:aws:s3:::your-bucket-name/*"
    }
  ]
}
```

2. Attaching IAM Roles to Lambda Functions

When you create a Lambda function, you can either use an existing IAM role or create a new one. To create a new role:

1. In the Lambda function configuration, choose **Execution role** under **Permissions**.
2. Select **Create a new role with basic Lambda permissions** (this role includes the basic permissions for Lambda execution).
3. To add additional permissions (e.g., for S3 access), you can either modify the role after creation or create a custom role with the specific permissions you need.

3. Managing IAM Policies for Lambda

You can use **IAM policies** to define what actions your Lambda function is allowed to perform on specific AWS services. These policies can be attached to IAM roles and specify the level of access (e.g., read-only, write, or full access) that the Lambda function should have.

Example of a restrictive policy that only allows read access to DynamoDB:

json
Copy

```json
{
    "Version": "2012-10-17",
    "Statement": [
        {
            "Effect": "Allow",
            "Action": "dynamodb:Query",
            "Resource": "arn:aws:dynamodb:region:account-id:table/your-table-name"
        }
    ]
}
```

4. Using Resource-based Policies for Lambda

For more granular control over Lambda execution, you can use **resource-based policies**. These policies define who can invoke your Lambda function and can be used in conjunction with IAM roles. For example, you can create a policy that allows only specific IAM users, services, or accounts to invoke your Lambda function.

Managing API Gateway Security: Authentication and Authorization

API Gateway is often used to expose AWS Lambda functions as HTTP endpoints. Since APIs are commonly accessible over the internet, securing them is vital. There are two main approaches to securing API Gateway endpoints: **authentication** and **authorization**.

1. API Gateway Authentication

Authentication ensures that only authorized users can access your API. API Gateway supports several ways to authenticate users:

- **API Key**: You can use API keys to restrict access to your API. While this method provides basic authentication, it is not highly secure, as anyone with the key can access your API.
  Example of enabling API key requirement:
    - In the **API Gateway Console**, under **Method Request**, set **API Key Required** to true.
    - Create an API key in the **API Keys** section and assign it to the method.
- **IAM Authentication**: API Gateway can also authenticate requests using **IAM roles and policies**. With IAM-based authentication, you can control which IAM

users or roles have permission to invoke the API.

Example:

- o **Lambda function invocation**: You can create an IAM policy to allow only specific IAM users to access the API.
- **Cognito User Pools**: Amazon **Cognito** can be used for user authentication, allowing users to sign in with social identities (Facebook, Google, etc.) or a custom identity provider. Once authenticated, users are granted a JWT (JSON Web Token) that can be used to authenticate API requests.

Example:

- o In API Gateway, configure a **Cognito Authorizer** under the **Authorization** settings of the API method.

2. API Gateway Authorization

Authorization ensures that authenticated users can only perform actions they are authorized to do. There are several ways to implement authorization in API Gateway:

- **Lambda Authorizers (Custom Authorizers)**: Lambda authorizers are custom Lambda functions that handle authorization logic. When a request is made, API Gateway invokes the Lambda authorizer to verify the token and ensure that the user has the correct permissions to access the resource.

Example:

- o Implement a Lambda function to verify JWT tokens passed in the Authorization header, and grant access based on the user's roles or claims.
- **Cognito Authorizers**: If you're using **Cognito** for user authentication, API Gateway can use **Cognito User Pools** for authorization. This simplifies the authorization process by allowing you to associate API methods with specific user roles in Cognito.

Example:

- ○ Create a **Cognito User Pool** in the **Cognito Console**, then link it to an API Gateway method to restrict access to users in specific groups.

Securing Serverless Applications with Environment Variables

Environment variables are commonly used to store sensitive information such as database credentials, API keys, and secret tokens. However, it's important to secure these environment variables to prevent unauthorized access.

1. Using Environment Variables in AWS Lambda

AWS Lambda allows you to define environment variables that can be accessed by your function code at runtime. These variables are useful for storing configuration settings and sensitive data that you don't want to hardcode into your code.

To set environment variables for your Lambda function:

1. Go to your **Lambda function's configuration page**.
2. Under **Environment variables**, click **Edit**.
3. Add key-value pairs for each environment variable (e.g., DB_PASSWORD = your-password).

These variables can be accessed from within your Lambda function:

python
Copy

```
import os

def lambda_handler(event, context):
    db_password = os.getenv('DB_PASSWORD')
    return {
```

```
'statusCode': 200,
'body': f'Password is: {db_password}'
}
```

2. Securing Environment Variables

While environment variables are convenient, they should be handled securely to avoid accidental exposure of sensitive information.

- **Encryption at Rest**: AWS automatically encrypts Lambda environment variables at rest. However, you can use **KMS (AWS Key Management Service)** to manage the encryption keys and ensure that your environment variables are securely encrypted.

  To enable KMS encryption:
  1. Go to the **Lambda Console** and select the function.
  2. Under **Environment variables**, choose **Enable encryption helpers**.

- **Access Control**: Use IAM policies to control which users and roles have access to Lambda functions and their environment variables. Be sure to follow the **principle of least privilege** by granting access only to those who need it.

Secure Secrets: For sensitive data, such as database credentials or API keys, avoid storing them as plain text in environment variables. Instead, use **AWS Secrets Manager** or **AWS Systems Manager Parameter Store** to store and retrieve secrets securely.

Example using **AWS Secrets Manager**:

python
Copy

```python
import boto3

def lambda_handler(event, context):
    secret_name = "my_secret"
    client = boto3.client('secretsmanager')
```

```
response = client.get_secret_value(SecretId=secret_name)
secret = response['SecretString']
return {
  'statusCode': 200,
  'body': f'Secret is: {secret}'
}
```

•

We covered the key aspects of securing serverless applications, including how to:

- Use **IAM roles and policies** to securely manage Lambda permissions and access to AWS resources.
- Implement **API Gateway authentication** and **authorization** mechanisms, including using API keys, IAM, and Cognito.
- Secure sensitive information in **Lambda environment variables,** and leverage services like **AWS Secrets Manager** for secure management of credentials.

By implementing these security measures, you can build more secure and resilient serverless applications, ensuring that only authorized users and systems can access your Lambda functions and sensitive data.

Data Encryption and Secure Communication

We will focus on securing data within serverless applications, particularly when using AWS Lambda. We'll cover the best practices for **data encryption**, including how to ensure that data is securely encrypted at rest and in transit. We'll also discuss how to implement **secure communication** between Lambda functions and other AWS services to protect sensitive information throughout its lifecycle.

99

Data Encryption and Secure Communication

Data security is a cornerstone of any application, and serverless applications are no exception. While AWS Lambda provides several built-in mechanisms to ensure data security, it is essential to implement proper encryption practices to safeguard sensitive data.

1. Data Encryption at Rest

Data at rest refers to any data that is stored on disk, whether in databases, storage systems like S3, or even Lambda environment variables. AWS provides automatic encryption mechanisms to help protect data at rest.

Encrypting Lambda Environment Variables: AWS Lambda automatically encrypts environment variables at rest, but you can manage encryption with AWS **KMS (Key Management Service)** for additional security. AWS KMS allows you to create and control encryption keys used to encrypt and decrypt data.

To enable KMS encryption for Lambda environment variables:

1. Open the Lambda function in the AWS Management Console.
2. Under the **Environment Variables** section, select **Enable encryption helpers**.
3. Choose a KMS key for encryption (you can use the default AWS-managed key or create your own).
4. After enabling encryption helpers, Lambda will encrypt the environment variables automatically at rest.

Encrypting Data in Amazon S3: Amazon S3 allows you to automatically encrypt objects when they are uploaded to a bucket, ensuring data is encrypted at rest. You can use either **S3-managed keys (SSE-S3), AWS Key Management Service (SSE-KMS)**, or **Customer-Provided Keys (SSE-C)**.

- **SSE-S3**: S3 automatically manages the encryption keys.
- **SSE-KMS**: You can use AWS KMS to manage encryption keys, providing more granular control over access to the encryption keys.

Example of enabling SSE-S3 encryption:

When uploading an object to S3, you can specify encryption using the put_object API.
python
Copy

```
s3 = boto3.client('s3')
s3.put_object(Bucket='my-bucket', Key='my-file.txt', Body='Hello, world!',
ServerSideEncryption='AES256')
```

1. **Encrypting Data in Amazon DynamoDB:** Amazon DynamoDB also encrypts data at rest by default. However, if you need to have more control over encryption, you can use **AWS KMS** to manage your own encryption keys for DynamoDB tables.

---

2. Data Encryption in Transit

Data in transit refers to any data that is actively moving through the network, such as data being transferred between services, clients, or Lambda functions. It's essential to secure this data to prevent unauthorized access or data breaches during transmission.

Encryption via HTTPS: When interacting with APIs or external services, always use **HTTPS** to ensure that data is encrypted in transit. If you're using API Gateway to expose Lambda functions as REST APIs, make sure that the API is accessible only through HTTPS.

Example of forcing HTTPS in API Gateway:

- In the **API Gateway console**, you can enforce the use of HTTPS by setting **Secure connection** for your API methods. This ensures that all communication is encrypted in transit.

Using TLS for Secure Communication: AWS services such as **S3, DynamoDB**, and **SNS** communicate securely using **TLS (Transport Layer Security)** by default. When calling these services from your Lambda functions, AWS automatically encrypts the data in transit using TLS, ensuring that your data remains secure while moving between services.

Example of using TLS in Lambda to connect to a remote service:

python
Copy

```
import requests

# Use HTTPS to ensure data is encrypted in transit
response = requests.get('https://example.com/api/data')
data = response.json()
```

Preventing and Handling Common Security Threats

In addition to encryption, it's essential to implement proper security measures to protect your Lambda functions and the data they handle from common security threats. In this section, we'll discuss some of the most common security threats in serverless applications and how to prevent and handle them.

---

1. AWS Lambda Security Best Practices

- **Minimize IAM Permissions (Principle of Least Privilege)**: The **principle of least privilege** means that you should grant only the necessary permissions for Lambda functions and IAM roles to perform their tasks. Overly permissive IAM roles can expose your application to unnecessary risks.
    - ○ **Example**: Instead of granting full access to an S3 bucket, only grant the GetObject permission if your function only needs to read objects.
- **Use IAM Roles for Lambda Execution**: Always use IAM roles to define the permissions needed for Lambda to access other AWS resources. Don't embed API keys or credentials in your Lambda function code. Use **IAM roles** for secure access to resources.

Use AWS Secrets Manager for Sensitive Data: AWS Secrets Manager allows you to store and manage sensitive data such as database credentials and API keys. Instead of embedding secrets in your Lambda code or environment variables, use Secrets Manager to securely retrieve them at runtime.

Example of using AWS Secrets Manager in Lambda:

python

Copy

```
import boto3

# Get the secret value from AWS Secrets Manager
secret_name = "my-database-credentials"
client = boto3.client('secretsmanager')
secret = client.get_secret_value(SecretId=secret_name)
credentials = secret['SecretString']
```

2. Preventing Denial of Service (DoS) Attacks

Lambda functions can be susceptible to Denial of Service (DoS) attacks, especially when exposed to the public via API Gateway. To prevent these attacks, take the following precautions:

- **Rate Limiting**: Use **API Gateway throttling** to limit the number of requests per second and prevent overloads from malicious actors. You can configure API Gateway to throttle requests to a set number per second or burst limit.
- **API Key Usage**: If your API is public, require API keys for access. This way, you can track and limit usage per key.
- **AWS WAF (Web Application Firewall)**: Use AWS WAF with API Gateway to protect your API from common web exploits like SQL injection or cross-site scripting (XSS) attacks. AWS WAF allows you to configure rules to block malicious traffic based on IP addresses, headers, or query parameters.

3. Protecting Against Injection Attacks

Injection attacks, such as **SQL Injection**, can occur when malicious data is sent to your Lambda function to execute harmful commands. To prevent these attacks:

- **Validate and Sanitize Inputs**: Always validate and sanitize input data to ensure that it doesn't contain malicious content. For example, validate that email addresses contain only valid characters and reject suspicious input.

Use Parameterized Queries: When interacting with databases, always use **parameterized queries** rather than building queries by concatenating user input. This prevents SQL injection attacks by separating query structure from data.
Example using **DynamoDB**:
python
Copy
response = table.query(

KeyConditionExpression=Key('email').eq('user@example.com')
)

- **Escaping Data**: Ensure that any data entered by users, particularly in query strings or URLs, is properly escaped before use in any database or external system. This protects your application from **cross-site scripting (XSS)** or **SQL injection** attacks.

4. Protecting Data at Rest and in Transit

While encryption in transit and at rest is crucial for protecting your data, it's important to ensure that only authorized users and applications can access that data. Here's how to secure your data:

- **Data Access Policies**: Define who can access your data at rest (in DynamoDB, S3, etc.) using **resource-based policies**. Use fine-grained access controls to grant access to only the necessary roles or users.
- **Encrypt Data in Transit**: Always use **HTTPS** for any external API calls or client-server communications. Use **TLS** (Transport Layer Security) to encrypt data in transit.

In this chapter, we covered essential security practices for protecting your serverless applications, particularly AWS Lambda. We explored how to:

- Secure **Lambda functions** using IAM roles and policies to follow the principle of least privilege.
- Protect **API Gateway** with authentication (via API keys, IAM, or Cognito) and authorization mechanisms (such as Lambda or Cognito authorizers).
- Safeguard sensitive data using **Lambda environment variables, AWS Secrets Manager**, and proper encryption methods.

- Prevent common security threats such as **Denial of Service (DoS)** attacks, **injection attacks**, and unauthorized data access.

By following these security best practices, you can ensure that your serverless applications remain secure, resilient, and compliant with best practices.

In the next chapter, we'll explore **advanced serverless patterns**, including using AWS Step Functions for orchestration, integrating machine learning into serverless applications, and more.

Chapter 8: Debugging and Troubleshooting Serverless Applications

Serverless applications, particularly those built with AWS Lambda, introduce new challenges when it comes to debugging and troubleshooting. Unlike traditional server-based applications, you don't have direct access to the underlying infrastructure or servers running your code. However, AWS provides a rich set of tools and best practices to help you debug Lambda functions effectively. In this chapter, we'll discuss the most common issues with AWS Lambda functions and how to troubleshoot them using **CloudWatch Logs** and other AWS tools.

Common Issues with AWS Lambda Functions

While AWS Lambda simplifies much of the infrastructure management, it can still be prone to a variety of issues. Understanding and identifying these problems early can save a lot of time and effort.

1. Cold Starts

A **cold start** occurs when AWS Lambda initializes a new instance of your function to handle a request. Cold starts can introduce significant latency, especially for larger functions or those with many dependencies. The function must load the runtime, dependencies, and any initialization code before executing the handler.

Symptoms:

- High response times for the first few requests after a period of inactivity.
- Performance degradation under inconsistent traffic patterns.

Solution:

- Minimize the size of your Lambda function's deployment package.
- Use **Lambda layers** to manage dependencies separately and reduce the size of the function.
- If low-latency response is critical, consider using **Provisioned Concurrency** to keep Lambda instances pre-warmed and ready to execute.

2. Function Timeout

By default, AWS Lambda functions have a timeout of **3 seconds**, but you can configure the timeout to be as long as **15 minutes**. A timeout occurs when the function exceeds the maximum execution time and is terminated by AWS.

Symptoms:

- The function doesn't return a result within the expected time frame.
- Errors indicating the function timed out.

Solution:

- Review your function's execution time and increase the timeout setting if necessary.
- Optimize your code to ensure that it completes more efficiently. This could include better algorithms, asynchronous processing, or reducing calls to external services.

3. Memory Issues

Lambda functions have a maximum memory allocation of **10 GB**. If your function requires more memory than it's allocated, it may fail with an error. Conversely, allocating too much memory might increase your costs unnecessarily.

Symptoms:

- Lambda functions fail with an **OutOfMemoryError**.

- Function performs poorly despite having a high timeout.

Solution:

- Review your function's memory usage with **CloudWatch metrics** to determine if the memory allocation is sufficient.
- Optimize your function to reduce memory consumption, such as by reducing data in-memory or using more efficient data structures.

4. Permission Errors (IAM Roles and Policies)

AWS Lambda functions rely on **IAM roles and policies** to interact with other AWS services. Incorrect or missing permissions can cause your Lambda function to fail when accessing resources such as S3, DynamoDB, or SNS.

Symptoms:

- Errors like **AccessDeniedException** or **UnauthorizedAccessException**.
- Your function fails to interact with other AWS services as expected.

Solution:

- Review the IAM role attached to your Lambda function to ensure it has the correct permissions.
- Use **IAM policy simulator** to test permissions for your Lambda function and ensure the role has the necessary access.

5. API Gateway Timeout or Throttling

If you are using AWS Lambda behind **API Gateway**, you may encounter issues like request timeouts or throttling errors due to high traffic or slow Lambda function execution.

Symptoms:

- **504 Gateway Timeout** errors when accessing the API.
- Throttling errors with HTTP status codes like **429 Too Many Requests**.

Solution:

- Increase the **timeout settings** in both API Gateway and Lambda.
- Use **API Gateway throttling** to limit the number of requests and avoid overload.
- Optimize Lambda function execution to reduce the overall execution time.

Debugging AWS Lambda with CloudWatch Logs

To troubleshoot and debug Lambda functions, **CloudWatch Logs** is one of the most useful tools provided by AWS. CloudWatch Logs automatically collects logs from your Lambda functions, giving you insight into how they are performing, identifying errors, and tracking performance over time.

1. Setting Up CloudWatch Logs

When you create a Lambda function, AWS automatically configures it to log function invocations to **CloudWatch Logs**. If you haven't already, ensure that your Lambda function has the necessary permissions to write logs to CloudWatch by attaching the **AWSLambdaBasicExecutionRole** policy to the function's IAM role.

Once your function is connected to CloudWatch Logs, you can view logs through the AWS Management Console:

- Navigate to **CloudWatch > Logs**.
- Find the **Log Group** for your Lambda function (it will be named /aws/lambda/{your-function-name}).

- Inside the log group, you will see **Log Streams**, which correspond to individual invocations of your Lambda function.

2. Using CloudWatch Logs for Debugging

CloudWatch Logs provide detailed information about each invocation of your Lambda function. You can leverage these logs to:

Track Function Execution: The logs capture detailed information about each Lambda invocation, including the event data, response, and errors.
Example log output:
json
Copy
```
{
  "statusCode": 200,
  "body": "Hello, Lambda!"
}
```

- **Identify Errors**: Lambda functions often log error messages if something goes wrong during execution. Look for the ERROR logs to identify issues in the function's behavior, such as missing data, permission issues, or connection failures.
  Example error message:
  vbnet
  Copy
  ```
  ERROR: Unhandled exception: KeyError: 'name'
  ```

- **Log Custom Data**: You can add custom log statements in your function's code to track specific parts of the execution flow or data processing.
  Example:
  python

Copy

```
import logging


def lambda_handler(event, context):
    logging.info('Received event: %s', event)
    try:
        # Your function logic here
    except Exception as e:
        logging.error('Error occurred: %s', e)
        raise
```

- **Monitoring Performance**: You can track the function's execution time by using log statements at the start and end of your function to measure how long it takes to complete. This can help you diagnose performance issues such as timeouts or inefficiencies.

  Example:

  python

  Copy

```
import time


def lambda_handler(event, context):
    start_time = time.time()
    # Function logic
    end_time = time.time()
    logging.info('Function execution time: %s seconds', end_time - start_time)
```

3. Analyzing Logs for Issues

Once your function's logs are available in CloudWatch, use the following strategies to analyze them:

- **Search and Filter Logs**: Use the **Filter** feature in CloudWatch Logs to search for specific terms, such as "error," "timeout," or custom log messages. This helps you focus on key issues without having to go through each individual log entry.

CloudWatch Insights: For more advanced log analysis, use **CloudWatch Logs Insights**, which allows you to run SQL-like queries on your logs to gain deeper insights. You can filter logs by parameters like function name, duration, or error message, making it easier to spot issues.

Example query to find logs with errors:

sql

Copy

```
fields @timestamp, @message
| filter @message like /ERROR/
| sort @timestamp desc
```

Common Lambda Errors and How to Handle Them

While debugging Lambda functions, you'll likely encounter some common errors. Let's take a look at a few of them and how to handle them effectively.

1. Timeout Errors

- **Cause**: The function is taking longer to execute than the allocated timeout.
- **Solution**: Increase the Lambda function timeout in the configuration or optimize your function to run faster. Consider breaking up long-running tasks into smaller, asynchronous operations.

2. Permission Errors

- **Cause**: Lambda doesn't have the necessary permissions to access AWS resources like S3, DynamoDB, or SNS.

- **Solution**: Check the IAM role attached to your Lambda function and ensure it has
- the correct permissions to access the required resources.

3. Missing Environment Variables

- **Cause**: Your Lambda function expects environment variables to be set (e.g., database credentials or API keys), but they are not present.
- **Solution**: Ensure the correct environment variables are set in the Lambda function configuration, and consider using AWS Secrets Manager to securely manage secrets.

4. Cold Start Latency

- **Cause**: The first invocation of a Lambda function after a period of inactivity takes longer than usual.
- **Solution**: Minimize function size and dependencies, or use **Provisioned Concurrency** to pre-warm Lambda instances to reduce cold start time.

We covered how to troubleshoot and debug AWS Lambda functions using **CloudWatch Logs**. We discussed common Lambda issues such as cold starts, timeouts, and permission errors, and provided solutions to help you address these problems. By utilizing CloudWatch Logs and other monitoring tools, you can gain valuable insights into your Lambda functions and optimize them for better performance and reliability.

Error Handling Strategies in Serverless Applications

Error handling is a critical aspect of building resilient and reliable serverless applications. In AWS Lambda, errors can occur due to various reasons such as misconfigurations, resource access issues, timeouts, and unexpected events. As serverless applications often involve multiple AWS services working together, understanding how to handle errors at each stage is essential. In this chapter, we will discuss various error handling strategies, including how to optimize Lambda cold starts and avoid Lambda function timeouts.

Error Handling Strategies in Serverless Applications

Error handling in serverless applications should not only address Lambda-specific issues but also handle errors that occur in the services interacting with Lambda functions, such as API Gateway, DynamoDB, and S3.

---

1. Using Try/Except for Lambda Functions

In Python, the try/except block is the most common way to handle errors. Lambda functions can throw exceptions, especially when interacting with external resources or facing runtime issues like null values or API failures. By wrapping the critical code in a try/except block, you can catch errors and take appropriate actions.

Example:

python

Copy

```
def lambda_handler(event, context):

    try:

        # Simulate code that may raise an exception

        result = 10 / event['number']

        return {
```

```python
            'statusCode': 200,

            'body': result

        }

    except KeyError:

        # Handle missing parameter

        return {

            'statusCode': 400,

            'body': 'Missing "number" parameter'

        }

    except ZeroDivisionError:

        # Handle division by zero error

        return {

            'statusCode': 400,

            'body': 'Cannot divide by zero'

        }

    except Exception as e:

        # Handle any other errors

        return {

            'statusCode': 500,
```

```
'body': f"An error occurred: {str(e)}"

}
```

In the above example, if the input event['number'] is missing or zero, the function will catch the specific errors and respond accordingly, preventing the function from failing entirely.

---

2. Dead Letter Queues (DLQ) for Failed Invocations

For Lambda functions that process asynchronous events, you can configure a **Dead Letter Queue (DLQ)** to capture failed invocations. If a Lambda function fails after multiple retries, the event can be sent to an Amazon SQS queue or an SNS topic for further investigation.

How DLQ Works:

- When Lambda cannot process an event after multiple retry attempts, the event is sent to a DLQ.
- This allows you to analyze the failure, reprocess the event, or trigger alarms for monitoring.

To set up a DLQ:

1. Go to the **Lambda function** configuration page.
2. In the **Asynchronous invocation** section, enable **Dead Letter Queue** and specify an SQS queue or SNS topic.
3. Configure retry and DLQ policies based on your needs.

---

3. Retry Strategies for Lambda Failures

Lambda automatically retries failed invocations for asynchronous events. However, you can control the **retry behavior** and **dead-lettering** using AWS services like **SNS, SQS,** and **Step Functions**.

- **Synchronous invocations** (e.g., via API Gateway) do not retry on failure by default.
- **Asynchronous invocations** (e.g., S3 event triggers) are retried twice, with a delay of a few minutes.

If a failure persists, the event is sent to a DLQ or an SNS topic, allowing you to inspect the event and take corrective action.

- **Use Step Functions**: If your Lambda functions need to be part of a larger workflow, **AWS Step Functions** can manage retries and define workflows that handle errors and retries explicitly.

---

4. Custom Error Handling Logic for Business Logic

In addition to system-level errors (e.g., network failures or resource issues), Lambda functions may encounter business logic errors. For instance, an order processing function might fail if the product is out of stock.

For these types of errors, you can implement custom error handling logic:

- **Custom Error Codes**: Return specific error codes or messages to notify clients of business rule violations. For example, a shopping cart service might return a "404 Not Found" status if a product is out of stock.
- **Fallback Logic**: If your Lambda function fails to process a request, you can implement fallback logic to try a secondary process, such as attempting a retry with different data or switching to a backup system.

Optimizing Lambda Cold Starts

Lambda functions are highly scalable and efficient, but one of the most common performance challenges is the **cold start**. A cold start occurs when a Lambda function is invoked for the first time after being idle or when a new container is spun up to handle the request. This introduces latency, which can negatively impact user experience, especially in real-time applications.

Let's explore how to minimize cold start latency and optimize Lambda functions for faster responses.

---

1. Minimize Function Package Size

Lambda functions experience longer cold starts if the deployment package is large, especially if it includes many unnecessary dependencies. By reducing the package size, you can speed up the cold start time.

- **Remove Unused Libraries**: Review the libraries included in your function and eliminate any that are not needed.
- **Use Lambda Layers**: If your function uses shared libraries, consider using **Lambda layers** to separate dependencies from the function code. This can make your Lambda function smaller and help reduce cold start times.
- **Example**: If your Lambda function uses the **requests** library, but only for a small part of the code, move it into a separate Lambda layer to minimize the function's size.

2. Use the Right Memory Allocation

AWS Lambda allocates more CPU power with higher memory allocation, which can help reduce cold start times. While higher memory configurations increase costs, they also improve performance, particularly for large functions with significant initialization overhead.

- **Benchmark Performance**: Test your Lambda function with different memory configurations to determine the optimal balance between performance and cost. Use **AWS Lambda Power Tuning** to automatically test different memory settings and optimize function performance.

3. Reduce Function Initialization Time

If your Lambda function has significant initialization logic (such as connecting to databases or loading configuration), this process will contribute to cold start latency. Try to:

- **Move Initialization Logic Outside the Handler**: Where possible, move any long-running initialization tasks outside the handler function to run during the cold start only. For example, if your function connects to a database, you can move the connection code to a global variable, which will be reused across function invocations.

Example:

python

Copy

```
# Initialize the database connection outside the handler to reuse it

db_connection = None
```

```
def lambda_handler(event, context):

    global db_connection

    if db_connection is None:

        db_connection = initialize_db_connection()


    # Your main function logic

    return {

        'statusCode': 200,

        'body': 'Database connection reused'

    }
```

4. Use Provisioned Concurrency

If your application requires **low-latency** performance, you can use **Provisioned Concurrency**. This feature keeps a specified number of Lambda instances pre-warmed and ready to execute requests, significantly reducing cold start times.

- **When to Use**: Use provisioned concurrency if you have predictable traffic and need consistent low latency, such as for APIs with high user engagement or mobile applications.
- **Cost Consideration**: While **Provisioned Concurrency** helps minimize cold starts, it comes with additional costs because you're essentially pre-allocating resources. Therefore, it's important to weigh the cost against the performance benefits.

Lambda Function Timeout: How to Avoid It

Lambda function timeouts can occur if the function execution exceeds the maximum allowed time. This can be caused by inefficient code, long-running processes, or slow dependencies (such as network calls).

To avoid timeouts, consider the following strategies:

---

1. Set the Right Timeout for Your Function

Each Lambda function has a configurable timeout setting. The default timeout is **3 seconds**, but this can be adjusted up to **15 minutes**.

- **Solution**: Review the expected execution time of your function and set the timeout accordingly. If your function requires more time due to external dependencies or complex logic, ensure the timeout reflects this.

Example:

python

Copy

```
# In the Lambda function console, set the timeout to an appropriate value
timeout_seconds = 10
```

2. Optimize Code Efficiency

One of the primary reasons for timeouts is inefficient code that takes longer to execute than expected. To reduce the likelihood of timeouts, optimize your code by:

- Reducing the number of external API calls (e.g., querying a database or interacting with third-party services).
- Minimizing complex computations inside the Lambda function.
- Avoiding blocking calls; instead, use asynchronous techniques or batch processing.

3. Use Asynchronous Processing for Long-Running Tasks

If your Lambda function performs long-running tasks, consider using **asynchronous invocations** or breaking the tasks into smaller chunks. For example, if a function needs to perform extensive data processing or call an external API multiple times, offload those tasks to another service or use **AWS Step Functions** to orchestrate them.

Example using **Step Functions** to break up tasks:

json

Copy

```
{

  "Comment": "A simple AWS Step Functions state machine",

  "StartAt": "ProcessData",

  "States": {

    "ProcessData": {

      "Type": "Task",

      "Resource": "arn:aws:lambda:REGION:ACCOUNT_ID:function:processData",

      "TimeoutSeconds": 60,

      "Next": "SendNotification"
```

```
    },

    "SendNotification": {

        "Type": "Task",

        "Resource": "arn:aws:lambda:REGION:ACCOUNT_ID:function:sendNotification",

        "End": true

    }

  }

}
```

This allows your application to handle long-running tasks without hitting the Lambda timeout limit.

In this chapter, we explored key strategies for **error handling** in serverless applications, including how to handle Lambda errors effectively using try/except blocks, dead-letter queues, and custom error logic. We also covered how to **minimize cold start latency** by optimizing memory allocation, reducing function size, and using **Provisioned Concurrency**.

Additionally, we discussed how to avoid **Lambda timeouts** by setting appropriate timeout values, optimizing code efficiency, and leveraging asynchronous processing or **AWS Step Functions** for long-running tasks.

By implementing these strategies, you can improve the reliability and performance of your Lambda functions, making your serverless applications more efficient and resilient.

In the next chapter, we will discuss **advanced serverless patterns** and dive into how to integrate machine learning models, use AWS Step Functions for orchestration, and build highly scalable serverless workflows.

Chapter 9: Real-World Project 1: Building a Serverless Todo List App

In this chapter, we will walk through a **real-world project**: building a **serverless Todo List application** using AWS Lambda and other AWS services. This project will allow you to apply the concepts and techniques you've learned so far to build a complete, fully-functional serverless application. The Todo List app will be simple but will demonstrate key principles such as using Lambda functions, API Gateway, DynamoDB, and more.

Let's start by introducing the project, the core features, and the design approach.

Introduction to the Project

Building a serverless Todo List application is a great way to demonstrate the power and flexibility of AWS Lambda in real-world applications. This project will highlight the following key concepts:

1. **Lambda Functions**: How to use AWS Lambda to handle the business logic of a serverless app.
2. **API Gateway**: How to expose Lambda functions via RESTful APIs for external interaction.
3. **DynamoDB**: How to use DynamoDB to persist user data.
4. **Authentication & Authorization**: How to secure the app using simple authentication methods.

By the end of this chapter, you will have a fully functional Todo List app that allows users to:

- Add new tasks to their todo list.
- View all tasks.
- Update the status of tasks.
- Delete tasks.

We will build the app step by step, focusing on each component of the serverless architecture.

Designing the Application: Overview and Features

The Todo List app will have a simple user interface (UI) that allows users to add, view, update, and delete tasks. These tasks will be stored in an **Amazon DynamoDB** table, and interactions will be handled by **AWS Lambda** functions exposed through **API Gateway**.

Core Features of the Todo List App

1. **Add a Task**: Users can create a new task by submitting a task description.
2. **View Tasks**: Users can retrieve and view all tasks in their list.
3. **Update a Task**: Users can mark tasks as completed or update their description.
4. **Delete a Task**: Users can remove tasks from their list.

In terms of serverless architecture, the app will consist of the following components:

1. **Lambda Functions**: We will have several Lambda functions, one for each of the CRUD operations (Create, Read, Update, Delete). Each function will handle the relevant API request, process the data, and interact with DynamoDB.
2. **API Gateway**: API Gateway will be used to expose Lambda functions as RESTful API endpoints. For example:
   - POST /tasks – Add a new task.
   - GET /tasks – Retrieve all tasks.

o PUT /tasks/{task_id} – Update the status or description of a task.

o DELETE /tasks/{task_id} – Delete a task.

3. **DynamoDB**: DynamoDB will be used to store the tasks. Each task will have an ID, description, and status (pending/completed).

Designing the Data Model (DynamoDB Table)

We will create a **DynamoDB table** to store the tasks. The table will have the following structure:

- **Table Name**: TodoListApp
- **Primary Key**:
  - **Partition Key**: task_id (String) – a unique identifier for each task.
- **Attributes**:
  - description (String) – The text or description of the task.
  - status (String) – The current status of the task (e.g., pending or completed).
  - created_at (String) – The timestamp when the task was created.
  - updated_at (String) – The timestamp of the last update to the task.

This table will be the heart of the Todo List app, storing all task data. The task_id will be the unique identifier for each task, and other attributes like status and description will allow users to interact with the task.

Application Flow Overview

Here's how the application will flow from a user's perspective:

1. **User Interactions with API Gateway**:
   o The user sends an HTTP request to one of the API endpoints via **API Gateway** (e.g., POST /tasks to add a task).

2. **Lambda Functions Handling the Requests**:
   - API Gateway routes the request to the corresponding **Lambda function**.
   - The Lambda function processes the request, interacts with **DynamoDB** to retrieve, add, update, or delete tasks, and then returns a response.
3. **Data Storage with DynamoDB**:
   - Each task will be stored in **DynamoDB** with the attributes specified earlier.
   - DynamoDB will serve as a highly scalable and low-latency database to store and retrieve tasks as users interact with the application.
4. **Response Sent to the User**:
   - After the Lambda function completes the task (e.g., adding a new task or fetching the list of tasks), it sends a response back to the user via **API Gateway**.

Technological Stack

To summarize, here's the technology stack we'll be using for this serverless Todo List app:

- **AWS Lambda**: For running the business logic of the application.
- **Amazon API Gateway**: For exposing Lambda functions as HTTP APIs.
- **Amazon DynamoDB**: For storing the tasks and their attributes.
- **AWS IAM**: For managing permissions to securely control access between Lambda functions and DynamoDB.
- **AWS CloudWatch Logs**: For monitoring and debugging the Lambda functions.

We introduced the **serverless Todo List app** project, providing an overview of the application's core features, the design of the data model, and the technologies that will be used to build the app. This application will help demonstrate how to integrate **AWS Lambda**, **API Gateway**, and **DynamoDB** to build a complete serverless application.

In the next section, we will start building the app, beginning with setting up the DynamoDB table and then creating the Lambda functions to handle CRUD operations. Each step will build on the concepts covered earlier in the book, allowing you to create a fully functional, serverless Todo List app.

Setting Up API Gateway and Lambda for CRUD Operations

Now that we have designed the Todo List app and understood the key components, we'll move on to the implementation. The first step is to set up the necessary AWS services, starting with **API Gateway** and **Lambda functions** for handling the CRUD (Create, Read, Update, and Delete) operations.

---

1. Setting Up API Gateway

API Gateway will serve as the front door for our serverless Todo List app. It will receive HTTP requests from users and route them to the corresponding AWS Lambda functions.

Here's how to set up API Gateway:

1. **Create an API Gateway REST API**:
   o Go to the **API Gateway** console and select **Create API**.
   o Choose **REST API** and click **Build**.
   o Set the **API name** (e.g., TodoListAPI) and description.
   o Click **Create API**.
2. **Create Resources and Methods**: We'll need four endpoints (methods) corresponding to the CRUD operations:
   o **POST /tasks**: To create a new task.
   o **GET /tasks**: To retrieve all tasks.

- PUT **/tasks/{task_id}**: To update a specific task.
- DELETE **/tasks/{task_id}**: To delete a task.

3. To create these endpoints:
    - In the **API Gateway Console**, select the newly created API.
    - Under **Resources**, select **Create Resource**.
        - Name the resource /tasks for the POST, GET, and DELETE methods.
        - For the PUT method, add {task_id} as a parameter in the resource path (e.g., /tasks/{task_id}).

4. **Configure Methods**: After creating the resources, configure each HTTP method:
    - For each method, click **Create Method** and choose **Lambda Function** as the integration type.
    - Select the Lambda function that corresponds to the action (e.g., **POST** method integrates with the Lambda function to create tasks).
    - Enable **Lambda Proxy Integration** for easier mapping of request/response.

5. **Deploy API**: Once all methods are created, you need to deploy the API:
    - In the **API Gateway Console**, click **Actions** > **Deploy API**.
    - Create a new **Stage** (e.g., dev) and click **Deploy**.
    - You will receive a **URL** for the API, which will be used to interact with your serverless application.

---

2. Setting Up Lambda Functions for CRUD Operations

Each CRUD operation will be handled by a separate AWS Lambda function. Let's go through the setup for each function.

1. **Create Lambda Functions**: Go to the **Lambda Console** and create the following functions:

- createTask: To handle creating new tasks.
- getTasks: To retrieve all tasks.
- updateTask: To update a task.
- deleteTask: To delete a task.
2. Each function will interact with **DynamoDB** to perform the relevant operations.

Lambda Code for Creating a Task: The createTask function will insert a new task into DynamoDB.

python

Copy

```python
import boto3

from datetime import datetime


# Initialize DynamoDB client

dynamodb = boto3.resource('dynamodb')

table = dynamodb.Table('TodoListApp')


def lambda_handler(event, context):

    task_id = str(datetime.timestamp(datetime.now()))  # Generate unique task ID

    task_description = event['body']['description']

    created_at = str(datetime.now())

    updated_at = created_at
```

```python
    # Insert task into DynamoDB

    table.put_item(

        Item={

            'task_id': task_id,

            'description': task_description,

            'status': 'pending',

            'created_at': created_at,

            'updated_at': updated_at

        }

    )


    return {

        'statusCode': 201,

        'body': f"Task with ID {task_id} created successfully"

    }
```

3. This function takes the task description from the event body and generates a unique task_id based on the current timestamp.

Lambda Code for Retrieving All Tasks: The getTasks function retrieves all tasks from DynamoDB.

python

Copy

```python
import boto3


# Initialize DynamoDB client

dynamodb = boto3.resource('dynamodb')

table = dynamodb.Table('TodoListApp')


def lambda_handler(event, context):

    # Scan the table to get all tasks

    response = table.scan()

    tasks = response.get('Items', [])


    return {

        'statusCode': 200,

        'body': {

            'tasks': tasks

        }

    }
```

4. This function performs a **scan** operation to retrieve all tasks from the TodoListApp **DynamoDB** table.

Lambda Code for Updating a Task: The updateTask function updates the task's status or description.

python

Copy

```python
import boto3


# Initialize DynamoDB client

dynamodb = boto3.resource('dynamodb')

table = dynamodb.Table('TodoListApp')


def lambda_handler(event, context):

    task_id = event['pathParameters']['task_id']

    description = event['body'].get('description', None)

    status = event['body'].get('status', None)

    updated_at = str(datetime.now())


    # Prepare the update expression

    update_expression = "SET updated_at = :updated_at"

    expression_attribute_values = {':updated_at': updated_at}


    if description:
```

```python
        update_expression += ", description = :description"

        expression_attribute_values[':description'] = description


    if status:

        update_expression += ", status = :status"

        expression_attribute_values[':status'] = status


    # Update the task in DynamoDB

    table.update_item(

        Key={'task_id': task_id},

        UpdateExpression=update_expression,

        ExpressionAttributeValues=expression_attribute_values

    )


    return {

        'statusCode': 200,

        'body': f"Task with ID {task_id} updated successfully"

    }
```

5. This function updates the description and/or status of the specified task identified by task_id.

Lambda Code for Deleting a Task: The deleteTask function removes a task from DynamoDB.

python

Copy

```python
import boto3


# Initialize DynamoDB client

dynamodb = boto3.resource('dynamodb')

table = dynamodb.Table('TodoListApp')


def lambda_handler(event, context):

    task_id = event['pathParameters']['task_id']


    # Delete the task from DynamoDB

    table.delete_item(

        Key={'task_id': task_id}

    )


    return {
```

'statusCode': 200,

'body': f"Task with ID {task_id} deleted successfully"

}

6. This function deletes the task from DynamoDB based on the task_id provided in the URL path.

Using DynamoDB as the Database Backend

Now that we've set up the Lambda functions and API Gateway, we will configure **DynamoDB** as the database backend to store our tasks. As we mentioned earlier, the table will have the following schema:

- **Table Name**: TodoListApp
- **Primary Key**:
  - **Partition Key**: task_id (String) – Unique identifier for each task.
- **Attributes**:
  - description (String) – Task description.
  - status (String) – Task status (pending or completed).
  - created_at (String) – Timestamp of task creation.
  - updated_at (String) – Timestamp of the last update.

1. **Creating the DynamoDB Table**:
   - Go to the **DynamoDB Console** and select **Create Table**.
   - Set the **Table name** to TodoListApp and the **Primary key** to task_id (String).
   - Leave other settings as default and create the table.

Testing and Deploying the Serverless Todo App

Now that everything is set up, let's test the serverless Todo List app to ensure all operations are functioning correctly.

1. **Test the API Methods**:
   - Use **Postman** or **curl** to send requests to the API Gateway endpoints.

POST /tasks: Send a JSON body to add a new task. Example:
json

Copy

```
{

  "description": "Buy groceries"

}
```

   -
   - **GET /tasks**: Send a request to retrieve all tasks.
   - **PUT /tasks/{task_id}**: Update a specific task by changing its description or status.
   - **DELETE /tasks/{task_id}**: Delete a specific task by its task_id.
2. **Deploying the Application**:
   - Ensure that your API is deployed by clicking on **Deploy API** in the API Gateway Console.
   - After deployment, API Gateway provides a URL that can be used to interact with the app.

In this chapter, we walked through the process of setting up **API Gateway**, creating **Lambda functions** for CRUD operations, and using **DynamoDB** as the database backend for the **serverless Todo List app**. We also covered how to test the application and deploy it using API Gateway.

In the next chapter, we will explore **monitoring** and **logging** for your serverless applications, and dive deeper into how to track performance and troubleshoot issues using AWS CloudWatch.

Chapter 10: Real-World Project 2: Building a Chatbot Using AWS Lex and Lambda

In this chapter, we'll explore how to build a **serverless chatbot** using **AWS Lex** and **AWS Lambda**. AWS Lex is a fully managed service that provides advanced natural language processing (NLP) and automatic speech recognition (ASR), enabling you to create conversational interfaces for your applications. Together with AWS Lambda, which will handle the business logic of the chatbot, we will design and build a fully functional serverless chatbot.

This project will give you hands-on experience in creating intelligent and scalable chatbots that can be integrated with various messaging platforms. Let's start by understanding **AWS Lex** and its role in serverless applications, and then we'll look at how to integrate **Python with AWS Lex** to build the chatbot's backend logic.

Introduction to AWS Lex and its Role in Serverless Applications

AWS Lex is a service that allows you to build conversational interfaces using voice and text. It integrates seamlessly with **AWS Lambda**, allowing you to add dynamic, data-driven responses to chatbot interactions. AWS Lex can handle tasks like:

1. **Natural Language Understanding (NLU)**: This enables the bot to understand user input, whether spoken or typed, and determine the intent behind the message.

2. **Automatic Speech Recognition (ASR)**: This allows the bot to understand and process speech, turning it into text that can be analyzed.

3. **Dialog Management**: AWS Lex provides tools to manage the flow of conversations, including collecting user input and managing multi-turn conversations.

AWS Lex is fully integrated with other AWS services like **Lambda, DynamoDB, SNS, and CloudWatch**, allowing you to create a serverless architecture where the chatbot's business logic is handled by AWS Lambda functions.

How AWS Lex Fits into Serverless Architectures

When building a serverless application, AWS Lex serves as the **front-end interface** that interacts with the user, while **AWS Lambda** acts as the **back-end** that processes the logic, queries databases, and sends back appropriate responses. This makes AWS Lex a great choice for integrating conversational interfaces into serverless applications.

Key benefits of using AWS Lex in serverless applications:

- **Cost Efficiency**: You only pay for the requests and speech processing time, so you're charged based on usage, making it a cost-effective solution for chatbots.
- **Scalability**: AWS Lex automatically scales to handle any volume of incoming requests, making it suitable for applications with varying traffic.
- **Integration with Other AWS Services**: AWS Lex can easily integrate with services like DynamoDB for data storage, Lambda for logic, and CloudWatch for monitoring.

Integrating Python with AWS Lex

Now that we've covered the basics of AWS Lex, let's dive into how to integrate **Python** with AWS Lex to handle the business logic of our chatbot using **AWS Lambda**.

1. Setting Up AWS Lex Bot

To build a chatbot, you'll first need to create an AWS Lex bot that can understand user input and trigger Lambda functions to handle responses.

- **Step 1: Create a Lex Bot**:
  - Go to the **AWS Lex Console** and click **Create Bot**.
  - Choose **Custom Bot** and give it a name (e.g., TodoBot for a task manager chatbot).
  - Set up the language and choose a voice (if you want the bot to speak to users).
  - Define **Intents**: An intent represents an action the user wants to take. For instance, a CreateTask intent could be used to create a new task.
  - For each intent, define **sample phrases** that users might say (e.g., "Add a new task", "Create a new to-do item").
- **Step 2: Create Intents and Sample Utterances**:
  - **Example Intent**: CreateTask
    - Sample Phrases:
      - "I need to create a new task"
      - "Add a task to my list"
  - **Example Intent**: GetTaskList
    - Sample Phrases:
      - "Show me my tasks"
      - "What tasks do I have?"
- **Step 3: Link Lambda Functions**: After defining your intents, you can integrate **Lambda functions** to process user input and respond accordingly. AWS Lex allows you to specify which Lambda function should be triggered for each intent. You'll write a Python function that will process the intent, interact with a database (e.g., DynamoDB), and return a response. You can use Lambda to fetch data, perform calculations, and send back dynamic responses.

2. Python Lambda Function for Chatbot Backend Logic

Let's look at how to write a Python Lambda function to handle the **CreateTask** intent in our chatbot.

Lambda Function for CreateTask **Intent**: Here, the Lambda function will take the task description from the user, store it in DynamoDB, and return a response confirming the task creation.

python

Copy

```python
import boto3
import json
from datetime import datetime

# Initialize DynamoDB client
dynamodb = boto3.resource('dynamodb')
table = dynamodb.Table('TodoListApp')

def lambda_handler(event, context):
    # Extract task description from Lex event
    task_description = event['currentIntent']['slots']['taskDescription']
    task_id = str(datetime.timestamp(datetime.now()))  # Generate a unique task ID
    created_at = str(datetime.now())

    # Insert task into DynamoDB
    table.put_item(
        Item={
            'task_id': task_id,
            'description': task_description,
            'status': 'pending',
```

```
        'created_at': created_at,
        'updated_at': created_at
    }
)


# Construct a message to send back to the user
message = f"Task '{task_description}' has been added to your list."


return {
    'dialogAction': {
        'type': 'Close',
        'fulfillmentState': 'Fulfilled',
        'message': {
            'contentType': 'PlainText',
            'content': message
        }
    }
}
```

Explanation:

- The function receives the user input (taskDescription) from the Lex event.
- It generates a unique task ID using the current timestamp.
- The task is inserted into DynamoDB, and a confirmation message is sent back to the user using Lex's **dialogAction**.

3. Handling Multiple Intents in Lambda

AWS Lex can trigger a Lambda function for multiple intents. You can handle different intents within a single Lambda function by checking the **intent name** in the event and executing different logic for each intent.

python

Copy

```python
def lambda_handler(event, context):
    intent_name = event['currentIntent']['name']

    if intent_name == 'CreateTask':
        return handle_create_task(event)
    elif intent_name == 'GetTaskList':
        return handle_get_task_list(event)
    else:
        return handle_unknown_intent(event)
```

In the above example, we check the intent name and call the corresponding handler function based on whether the user wants to create a task, retrieve the task list, or handle an unknown intent.

4. Handling Slots and Parameters in Lambda

AWS Lex allows you to define **slots** for capturing parameters in user input. For example, in the CreateTask intent, you might define a slot for the task description.

When AWS Lex passes the event to Lambda, the **slots** will be part of the event, and you can extract their values.

Example of extracting a slot value:

python

Copy

```python
task_description = event['currentIntent']['slots']['taskDescription']
```

You can use these slot values to perform actions based on user input. For example, you might want to validate the task description to ensure it's not empty or handle invalid input.

Building a Serverless Chatbot: Key Concepts

Building a serverless chatbot involves understanding how the various AWS services (Lex, Lambda, DynamoDB) work together. Here's a recap of the key concepts involved:

1. **AWS Lex**: Acts as the interface for interacting with the user. It captures user input and maps it to intents, triggering Lambda functions based on user requests.
2. **AWS Lambda**: Processes the business logic for the chatbot, such as interacting with databases (DynamoDB), calling APIs, and formatting responses. Lambda is the core of the backend for the chatbot.
3. **DynamoDB**: Serves as the data store where user input (e.g., tasks) is saved. DynamoDB is highly scalable, ensuring that even as your chatbot scales, it can handle large amounts of data efficiently.
4. **API Gateway**: If the chatbot needs to be exposed as a RESTful API or integrated with other platforms (e.g., Facebook Messenger, Slack), **API Gateway** can be used to expose AWS Lambda functions via HTTP endpoints.
5. **Slot Management**: Lex uses slots to capture specific pieces of information from user input (e.g., task description). Lambda can access these slot values to perform the necessary logic and respond accordingly.
6. **Dialog Management**: Lex manages the flow of conversations. It helps ensure that the chatbot asks the right questions, responds to user input, and handles multi-turn conversations smoothly.

We introduced the concept of building a **serverless chatbot** using **AWS Lex** and **AWS Lambda**. We covered:

- The role of AWS Lex in serverless applications and how it helps build conversational interfaces.
- How to integrate **Python** with **AWS Lex** by using **Lambda functions** to process intents.
- Key concepts for building the chatbot's backend, including DynamoDB for data storage and Lambda for business logic.

Creating Lambda Functions to Handle Chatbot Requests

Now that we have a basic understanding of AWS Lex and how it interacts with Lambda, we'll focus on the actual **Lambda functions** that handle requests from the user and manage the chatbot's behavior. These Lambda functions will process the user's input, interact with DynamoDB to retrieve or store data, and then return appropriate responses to the user.

---

1. Lambda Function to Handle "CreateTask" Intent

The CreateTask intent is triggered when a user asks the chatbot to create a new task. The Lambda function for this intent will insert a new task into **DynamoDB** and return a confirmation message to the user.

Here's how the Lambda function for the CreateTask intent might look:

python
Copy
```
import boto3
from datetime import datetime
```

```python
# Initialize DynamoDB client
dynamodb = boto3.resource('dynamodb')
table = dynamodb.Table('TodoListApp')

def lambda_handler(event, context):
    # Extract task description from Lex event slots
    task_description = event['currentIntent']['slots']['taskDescription']

    # Generate a unique task ID and timestamp
    task_id = str(datetime.timestamp(datetime.now()))  # Using timestamp as task ID
    created_at = str(datetime.now())
    updated_at = created_at

    # Insert the task into DynamoDB
    table.put_item(
        Item={
            'task_id': task_id,
            'description': task_description,
            'status': 'pending',
            'created_at': created_at,
            'updated_at': updated_at
        }
    )

    # Construct a message to send back to the user
    message = f"Task '{task_description}' has been added to your list."

    # Return the message to Lex
    return {
        'dialogAction': {
```

```
'type': 'Close',
'fulfillmentState': 'Fulfilled',
'message': {
    'contentType': 'PlainText',
    'content': message
}
}
}
```

Explanation:

- The function extracts the taskDescription slot from the event received from AWS Lex.
- It generates a unique task_id based on the current timestamp and creates the task in DynamoDB.
- A confirmation message is returned to the user indicating that the task has been successfully added.

---

2. Lambda Function to Handle "GetTaskList" Intent

Next, let's create the Lambda function that will retrieve and display a list of tasks from **DynamoDB** when the user asks to see their tasks. This intent will fetch all tasks and return them in a readable format.

python
Copy
```python
import boto3

# Initialize DynamoDB client
```

```python
dynamodb = boto3.resource('dynamodb')
table = dynamodb.Table('TodoListApp')

def lambda_handler(event, context):
    # Retrieve all tasks from DynamoDB
    response = table.scan()
    tasks = response.get('Items', [])

    # Construct the message to return the list of tasks
    if tasks:
        task_list = "\n".join([f"{task['description']} - {task['status']}" for task in tasks])
        message = f"Here are your tasks:\n{task_list}"
    else:
        message = "You have no tasks at the moment."

    # Return the message to Lex
    return {
        'dialogAction': {
            'type': 'Close',
            'fulfillmentState': 'Fulfilled',
            'message': {
                'contentType': 'PlainText',
                'content': message
            }
        }
    }
```

Explanation:

- The function uses the scan operation on the DynamoDB table to retrieve all tasks stored in the TodoListApp table.
- It formats the list of tasks into a readable string and returns it to the user as part of the response message.
- If there are no tasks, it lets the user know that their task list is empty.

---

3. Lambda Function to Handle "UpdateTask" Intent

The UpdateTask intent will be used to update the status or description of an existing task. For example, if the user wants to mark a task as completed or change the task's description, this Lambda function will process those requests.

python
Copy

```python
import boto3
from datetime import datetime

# Initialize DynamoDB client
dynamodb = boto3.resource('dynamodb')
table = dynamodb.Table('TodoListApp')

def lambda_handler(event, context):
    # Extract task_id and new values from Lex event
    task_id = event['currentIntent']['slots']['task_id']
    new_description = event['currentIntent']['slots']['newDescription']
    new_status = event['currentIntent']['slots']['newStatus']
    updated_at = str(datetime.now())
```

```python
# Prepare the update expression
update_expression = "SET updated_at = :updated_at"
expression_attribute_values = {':updated_at': updated_at}

if new_description:
    update_expression += ", description = :new_description"
    expression_attribute_values[':new_description'] = new_description

if new_status:
    update_expression += ", status = :new_status"
    expression_attribute_values[':new_status'] = new_status

# Update the task in DynamoDB
table.update_item(
    Key={'task_id': task_id},
    UpdateExpression=update_expression,
    ExpressionAttributeValues=expression_attribute_values
)

# Construct a message to return to the user
message = f"Task {task_id} has been updated."

# Return the message to Lex
return {
    'dialogAction': {
        'type': 'Close',
        'fulfillmentState': 'Fulfilled',
        'message': {
            'contentType': 'PlainText',
            'content': message
```

```
            }
        }
    }
```

Explanation:

- This function updates the description and/or status of a task in DynamoDB.
- It uses an **update expression** to modify the task attributes based on the user input (new description or new status).
- After the update, a confirmation message is returned to the user.

---

4. Lambda Function to Handle "DeleteTask" Intent

The DeleteTask intent will delete a specific task from DynamoDB. When the user asks to delete a task, the Lambda function will remove the task from the database.

python
Copy
```python
import boto3

# Initialize DynamoDB client
dynamodb = boto3.resource('dynamodb')
table = dynamodb.Table('TodoListApp')

def lambda_handler(event, context):
    # Extract task_id from Lex event
    task_id = event['currentIntent']['slots']['task_id']

    # Delete the task from DynamoDB
    table.delete_item(
```

```
    Key={'task_id': task_id}
)


# Construct a message to return to the user
message = f"Task {task_id} has been deleted."


# Return the message to Lex
return {
   'dialogAction': {
      'type': 'Close',
      'fulfillmentState': 'Fulfilled',
      'message': {
         'contentType': 'PlainText',
         'content': message
      }
   }
}
```

Explanation:

- The function extracts the task_id from the user input and deletes the corresponding task from DynamoDB using the delete_item method.
- A confirmation message is returned to the user to indicate that the task was successfully deleted.

Deploying and Testing the Chatbot

Now that we've set up the Lambda functions for all the intents, let's proceed with **deploying** and **testing** the chatbot.

1. Deploying the Lex Bot

Once the intents and Lambda functions are connected, you need to deploy the **AWS Lex Bot**.

1. In the **AWS Lex Console**, click on your bot and select **Build** to compile the changes.
2. After building the bot, go to **Test Chatbot**.
3. In the test interface, you can now start interacting with your chatbot by typing messages like "Add a new task" or "What tasks do I have?" and Lex will call the corresponding Lambda functions.

2. Testing the Lambda Functions

- **Test CreateTask**: Send a message like **"Add a new task: Buy groceries"** to the bot and check if the task is created successfully in DynamoDB.
- **Test GetTaskList**: Ask the bot **"What tasks do I have?"** to ensure it retrieves the list of tasks.
- **Test UpdateTask**: Use a message like **"Update task 1 to complete"** to check if the task is updated correctly.
- **Test DeleteTask**: Ask the bot **"Delete task 1"** to see if the task is removed from DynamoDB.

3. Deploying the Chatbot to Production

Once testing is complete and the chatbot is functioning as expected, you can deploy the bot for production use:

1. **Enable Webhooks**: If you plan to use the chatbot in a web interface or integrate it with other platforms (Slack, Facebook Messenger), set up **AWS API Gateway** to expose your Lex bot as an HTTP endpoint.
2. **Set up integrations**: AWS Lex integrates with messaging platforms like **Slack**, **Facebook Messenger**, and **Twilio SMS**, allowing you to use the chatbot across multiple channels.

In this chapter, we walked through the process of building a serverless chatbot using **AWS Lex** and **AWS Lambda**. We created Lambda functions to handle different intents, such as **CreateTask**, **GetTaskList**, **UpdateTask**, and **DeleteTask**, and integrated them with AWS Lex to provide a conversational interface for managing tasks.

We also covered the process of deploying and testing the chatbot, and discussed how to integrate it with other platforms using **API Gateway**. By building this chatbot, you've gained practical experience in using **AWS Lex**, **AWS Lambda**, and **DynamoDB** to create scalable, serverless applications.

Chapter 11: Advanced Serverless Patterns with Python

In this chapter, we'll explore advanced serverless patterns and architectures that leverage AWS Lambda and Python for building scalable, reliable, and real-time serverless applications. Specifically, we'll dive into **Microservices Architecture with AWS Lambda and Python** and explore the power of **Event-Driven Architectures for Real-Time Data Processing**. These patterns are essential for building complex serverless applications that require decoupling, scalability, and real-time data handling.

Microservices Architecture with AWS Lambda and Python

A **microservices architecture** is an approach to building applications as a set of loosely coupled, independently deployable services. Each service in a microservices architecture is typically responsible for a specific business function, and it communicates with other services using APIs.

AWS Lambda fits perfectly within a microservices architecture because it allows each microservice to run independently and scale automatically based on demand, without the need to manage infrastructure. In this section, we'll discuss how to build microservices using AWS Lambda and Python, and how to orchestrate these services effectively.

1. What is Microservices Architecture?

In a traditional monolithic application, all components (such as the user interface, business logic, and data access layer) are tightly integrated and run as a single unit. In contrast, a **microservices** approach divides the application into multiple, smaller services, each with its own functionality and independent lifecycle.

- **Decoupling**: Microservices allow for greater flexibility, enabling independent scaling and development cycles for each service.
- **Fault Isolation**: Failures in one service do not necessarily affect other services.
- **Technology Independence**: Different services can be built with different technologies or programming languages, such as Python, Node.js, or Java.

2. Building Microservices with AWS Lambda and Python

Each AWS Lambda function can be treated as an individual microservice. AWS Lambda provides a stateless execution environment where each function can handle a specific task or service. Here's an example of how you could break down a simple e-commerce application into microservices:

- **Product Service**: Handles product information, such as adding and updating products.
- **Order Service**: Handles the creation of orders and updating their status.
- **Inventory Service**: Manages inventory levels and stock availability.
- **Payment Service**: Manages payment processing for orders.

Each of these services will be implemented as separate Lambda functions that communicate with each other via API Gateway or event-driven mechanisms.

3. Example: Microservices for an E-Commerce Application

Let's illustrate how microservices architecture can be applied using **AWS Lambda** and **Python** for an e-commerce app that manages products, orders, and payments.

Product Service: This Lambda function manages products. It handles creating new products, updating product details, and deleting products.

python

Copy

```
import boto3
from datetime import datetime
```

```python
# Initialize DynamoDB client
dynamodb = boto3.resource('dynamodb')
table = dynamodb.Table('ProductCatalog')

def lambda_handler(event, context):
    # Extract product details from the event
    product_id = event['product_id']
    product_name = event['product_name']
    price = event['price']

    # Insert the product into DynamoDB
    table.put_item(
        Item={
            'product_id': product_id,
            'product_name': product_name,
            'price': price,
            'created_at': str(datetime.now())
        }
    )

    return {
        'statusCode': 201,
        'body': f"Product '{product_name}' created successfully."
    }
```

- **Order Service**: This Lambda function creates orders. It stores order details and communicates with the payment service to process the payment.
  python

Copy

```python
import boto3

# Initialize DynamoDB client
dynamodb = boto3.resource('dynamodb')
table = dynamodb.Table('Orders')

def lambda_handler(event, context):
    # Extract order details from event
    order_id = event['order_id']
    customer_id = event['customer_id']
    product_id = event['product_id']
    status = 'pending'

    # Create the order in DynamoDB
    table.put_item(
        Item={
            'order_id': order_id,
            'customer_id': customer_id,
            'product_id': product_id,
            'status': status
        }
    )

    # Here, you would invoke the payment service to process the payment

    return {
        'statusCode': 201,
        'body': f"Order '{order_id}' created successfully."
```

}

- **Payment Service**: This Lambda function processes payments. It could integrate with third-party payment gateways and handle payment status updates.

python

Copy

```python
import boto3


def lambda_handler(event, context):
    # Simulate payment processing
    payment_status = "success"  # In a real-world scenario, this would be based on an API call

    # Update order status based on payment result
    dynamodb = boto3.resource('dynamodb')
    table = dynamodb.Table('Orders')
    table.update_item(
        Key={'order_id': event['order_id']},
        UpdateExpression="SET status = :status",
        ExpressionAttributeValues={':status': payment_status}
    )

    return {
        'statusCode': 200,
        'body': f"Payment processed for order {event['order_id']}. Status: {payment_status}"
    }
```

4. Orchestrating Microservices with AWS Step Functions

In a real-world microservices architecture, these services often need to be orchestrated to complete a series of tasks in a specific order. **AWS Step Functions** is a service that allows you to coordinate multiple AWS Lambda functions into serverless workflows, helping you manage dependencies between services.

For instance, when a user creates an order, Step Functions can orchestrate the following flow:

1. Call the **Order Service** to create the order.
2. Call the **Payment Service** to process the payment.
3. Update the **Order Status** in the DynamoDB table.

Here's an example of a **Step Functions** workflow that handles the order processing:

json
Copy

```json
{
  "StartAt": "CreateOrder",
  "States": {
    "CreateOrder": {
      "Type": "Task",
      "Resource": "arn:aws:lambda:REGION:ACCOUNT_ID:function:createOrder",
      "Next": "ProcessPayment"
    },
    "ProcessPayment": {
      "Type": "Task",
      "Resource": "arn:aws:lambda:REGION:ACCOUNT_ID:function:processPayment",
      "End": true
    }
  }
}
```

Event-Driven Architectures: Real-Time Data Processing

Event-driven architectures are ideal for serverless applications because they enable efficient processing of events as they occur. In such architectures, the system reacts to events in real-time, typically by invoking Lambda functions to process the events.

1. Real-Time Event Processing with AWS Lambda

AWS Lambda can be triggered by a variety of event sources, such as:

- **DynamoDB Streams**: Automatically trigger Lambda functions when data changes in DynamoDB.
- **S3 Event Notifications**: Invoke a Lambda function when an object is uploaded to an S3 bucket.
- **SNS (Simple Notification Service)**: Trigger Lambda functions when an SNS topic receives a message.
- **Kinesis Streams**: Process streaming data in real time, such as user interactions or financial transactions.

2. Example: Real-Time Order Processing System

Let's build a simple **real-time order processing** system using **AWS Lambda** and **DynamoDB Streams**.

- **DynamoDB Streams** will capture changes to the Orders table, such as new orders or updates to order status.
- A Lambda function will be triggered by these stream events to process the order and send notifications.

```python
Copy
import boto3

# Initialize SNS client
sns = boto3.client('sns')

def lambda_handler(event, context):
    # Extract the order data from the DynamoDB stream event
    for record in event['Records']:
        if record['eventName'] == 'INSERT':
            new_order = record['dynamodb']['NewImage']
            order_id = new_order['order_id']['S']
            status = new_order['status']['S']

            # Process the new order (e.g., initiate payment or confirm shipment)
            message = f"New order received: {order_id}, Status: {status}"

            # Send a notification via SNS
            sns.publish(
                TopicArn='arn:aws:sns:REGION:ACCOUNT_ID:orderTopic',
                Message=message,
                Subject='New Order Notification'
            )

    return {
        'statusCode': 200,
        'body': 'Order processed successfully'
    }
```

In this example, when a new order is inserted into the DynamoDB table, the Lambda function is triggered by the stream event. The Lambda function processes the event and sends a notification via **SNS**.

3. Benefits of Event-Driven Architectures

Event-driven architectures offer several advantages in serverless applications:

- **Scalability**: Events trigger Lambda functions, which automatically scale in response to demand.
- **Loose Coupling**: Components of the system can operate independently, reacting to events without relying on synchronous calls.
- **Real-Time Processing**: Events are processed as soon as they occur, making the system highly responsive.

We explored advanced serverless patterns, including **Microservices Architecture** and **Event-Driven Architectures**, using **AWS Lambda** and **Python**. We learned how to break down applications into independent microservices, each managed by its own Lambda function, and how to use **AWS Step Functions** to orchestrate multiple services.

We also delved into **real-time data processing** by using event-driven architectures, specifically leveraging **DynamoDB Streams**, **SNS**, and **Lambda** to build scalable and responsive systems.

As you move forward, these advanced patterns will help you design and implement robust, scalable, and real-time serverless applications that can handle complex workflows and large volumes of data with minimal infrastructure management.

Managing State in Serverless Applications

We will explore key concepts and advanced patterns in serverless applications, specifically **managing state** in serverless applications using **AWS Step Functions**, leveraging **serverless machine learning** with **AWS Lambda** and **Python**, and creating **advanced API designs** with **Lambda** and **API Gateway**. These topics will enhance your understanding of how to manage complex workflows, integrate machine learning models, and design APIs in a scalable and serverless environment.

Managing State in Serverless Applications (Step Functions)

In serverless applications, one of the key challenges is managing state across different services and function invocations. Unlike traditional monolithic architectures, serverless functions are stateless by nature. However, in many cases, maintaining state across various function calls is necessary. **AWS Step Functions** allows you to manage state in a serverless environment by orchestrating a sequence of Lambda functions.

1. What Are AWS Step Functions?

AWS Step Functions is a fully managed service that allows you to coordinate multiple AWS services into serverless workflows. You can design workflows that involve AWS Lambda functions, AWS Batch, DynamoDB, and other services, all while handling state, retries, error handling, and parallel execution.

Key Features:

- **State Management**: Step Functions enables you to manage the state of your application by passing data between different Lambda functions and services.
- **Error Handling and Retries**: Automatically retry failed tasks and catch errors during execution.

- **Parallel Execution**: Execute multiple tasks simultaneously to speed up workflows.
- **Visual Workflow**: Step Functions provides a graphical interface to design workflows, making it easy to visualize and manage.

2. Example: Managing State with Step Functions

Let's consider a scenario where we need to process an order in a serverless application. The workflow could include:

1. **Step 1**: Validate the order.
2. **Step 2**: Process payment.
3. **Step 3**: Update inventory.
4. **Step 4**: Notify the user.

Using **AWS Step Functions**, we can create a state machine that orchestrates these tasks.

Step Functions Workflow Example:

json
Copy

```
{
  "StartAt": "ValidateOrder",
  "States": {
    "ValidateOrder": {
      "Type": "Task",
      "Resource": "arn:aws:lambda:REGION:ACCOUNT_ID:function:validateOrder",
      "Next": "ProcessPayment"
    },
    "ProcessPayment": {
      "Type": "Task",
      "Resource": "arn:aws:lambda:REGION:ACCOUNT_ID:function:processPayment",
```

```
    "Next": "UpdateInventory"
  },
  "UpdateInventory": {
    "Type": "Task",
    "Resource": "arn:aws:lambda:REGION:ACCOUNT_ID:function:updateInventory",
    "Next": "NotifyUser"
  },
  "NotifyUser": {
    "Type": "Task",
    "Resource": "arn:aws:lambda:REGION:ACCOUNT_ID:function:notifyUser",
    "End": true
  }
 }
}
```

In the example above, Step Functions coordinates each Lambda function to perform a specific task in the order, managing the state of each operation and passing data between functions.

3. Advantages of Using Step Functions for State Management

- **Decoupling**: Step Functions decouples tasks, allowing each task to be independent.
- **Error Handling**: You can define custom error handling strategies, such as retrying on failure or sending alerts if something goes wrong.
- **State Preservation**: Step Functions preserves the state of each task, so you don't have to worry about handling state manually between Lambda function invocations.

Serverless Machine Learning with AWS Lambda and Python

Serverless architectures can also integrate machine learning models to add intelligence to your applications. **AWS Lambda** provides a highly scalable environment to deploy machine learning models, allowing you to run inference without managing the underlying infrastructure.

1. Using AWS Lambda for Machine Learning Inference

AWS Lambda can invoke machine learning models directly or through **Amazon SageMaker** for inference. You can deploy machine learning models in Lambda by including them in your function's deployment package or by using SageMaker endpoints to invoke the models for predictions.

Example: Suppose you have a machine learning model for sentiment analysis. You can invoke this model from a Lambda function that processes incoming data in real time.

2. Example: Sentiment Analysis with AWS Lambda

Let's walk through how to use **AWS Lambda** for sentiment analysis by integrating with a pre-trained model in **Amazon SageMaker.**

- **Step 1**: Train and deploy a sentiment analysis model using **Amazon SageMaker.**
- **Step 2**: Use **AWS Lambda** to invoke the SageMaker endpoint to run inference on new text input.

Here's an example Lambda function in Python that invokes the sentiment analysis model:

```python
Copy
import boto3
```

```python
import json

# Initialize the SageMaker runtime client
sagemaker_runtime = boto3.client('runtime.sagemaker')

def lambda_handler(event, context):
    # Extract the text from the event (e.g., user input)
    text_input = event['text_input']

    # Invoke the SageMaker endpoint for sentiment analysis
    response = sagemaker_runtime.invoke_endpoint(
        EndpointName='SentimentAnalysisEndpoint',
        ContentType='application/json',
        Body=json.dumps({"text": text_input})
    )

    # Extract the sentiment prediction
    result = json.loads(response['Body'].read().decode())
    sentiment = result['predicted_class']

    return {
        'statusCode': 200,
        'body': f"Sentiment: {sentiment}"
    }
```

Explanation:

- This Lambda function takes a text input (e.g., a user's message), sends it to a **SageMaker endpoint** for sentiment analysis, and returns the predicted sentiment.

171

3. Benefits of Serverless Machine Learning with Lambda

- **Cost-Effective**: Only pay for the compute time when the function is invoked.
- **Scalable**: AWS Lambda scales automatically to handle high volumes of inference requests.
- **No Infrastructure Management**: Lambda abstracts away the infrastructure management, allowing you to focus solely on the model and inference logic.

Advanced API Design with Lambda, API Gateway, and Python

In many serverless applications, **API Gateway** is used to expose Lambda functions as RESTful APIs. However, as your application grows, you may need to implement **advanced API design** patterns to handle complex use cases, such as security, versioning, rate limiting, and multi-step workflows.

1. Designing Advanced APIs with API Gateway and Lambda

API Gateway is a powerful tool for exposing your Lambda functions to the web or other services. When designing advanced APIs, you may need to consider the following:

- **Versioning**: API versioning helps manage changes to your API while ensuring backward compatibility.
- **Rate Limiting**: Protect your API by setting usage plans and throttling limits to prevent abuse.
- **Request Validation**: Use API Gateway to validate incoming requests, ensuring they adhere to your schema.

2. Example: Advanced API Design with API Gateway and Lambda

Let's implement an API where users can access and update their profiles. This API will involve multiple steps:

1. **GET /profile/{user_id}** – Retrieve a user profile.
2. **PUT /profile/{user_id}** – Update a user profile.

To handle these operations, we'll set up API Gateway to route requests to Lambda functions.

Lambda Function for GET /profile/{user_id}:

python
Copy
```python
import boto3

# Initialize DynamoDB client
dynamodb = boto3.resource('dynamodb')
table = dynamodb.Table('UserProfiles')

def lambda_handler(event, context):
    user_id = event['pathParameters']['user_id']

    # Get the user profile from DynamoDB
    response = table.get_item(Key={'user_id': user_id})
    user_profile = response.get('Item', None)

    if user_profile:
        return {
            'statusCode': 200,
            'body': json.dumps(user_profile)
```

```python
        }
    else:
        return {
            'statusCode': 404,
            'body': 'User not found'
        }
```

Lambda Function for PUT /profile/{user_id}:

python
Copy
```python
import boto3
import json

# Initialize DynamoDB client
dynamodb = boto3.resource('dynamodb')
table = dynamodb.Table('UserProfiles')

def lambda_handler(event, context):
    user_id = event['pathParameters']['user_id']
    user_data = json.loads(event['body'])

    # Update the user profile in DynamoDB
    table.update_item(
        Key={'user_id': user_id},
        UpdateExpression="SET name = :name, email = :email",
        ExpressionAttributeValues={
            ':name': user_data['name'],
            ':email': user_data['email']
        }
```

174

```
)

return {
    'statusCode': 200,
    'body': 'Profile updated successfully'
}
```

Explanation:

- The GET /profile/{user_id} endpoint retrieves the user profile from DynamoDB.
- The PUT /profile/{user_id} endpoint updates the user profile in DynamoDB.

3. Best Practices for Advanced API Design

- **Versioning**: Implement API versioning by creating new API Gateway stages for each version.
- **Security**: Use **Cognito** for user authentication and **IAM** roles for authorization.
- **Rate Limiting**: Set up usage plans in API Gateway to limit the number of requests per user.

In this chapter, we explored advanced serverless patterns using **AWS Lambda** and **Python**. We learned how to:

- Use **AWS Step Functions** to manage state and orchestrate workflows in serverless applications.
- Integrate **serverless machine learning** into applications by invoking **SageMaker** endpoints from Lambda.
- Design **advanced APIs** with **Lambda** and **API Gateway**, including multi-step workflows, request validation, versioning, and rate limiting.

175

These advanced patterns will help you build more robust, scalable, and maintainable serverless applications, enabling you to manage complex workflows and integrate machine learning capabilities seamlessly.

Chapter 12: Managing and Monitoring Serverless Applications

In this chapter, we will explore how to effectively manage and monitor serverless applications, focusing on AWS Lambda. **AWS CloudWatch** plays a central role in this process by providing tools for monitoring, logging, and troubleshooting Lambda functions. We'll dive into using **CloudWatch for monitoring Lambda functions**, creating **custom metrics and alerts**, and troubleshooting Lambda failures with **CloudWatch Insights**. Monitoring is crucial for ensuring the health, performance, and reliability of serverless applications, so let's get started.

Using AWS CloudWatch for Monitoring Lambda Functions

AWS CloudWatch is a powerful service that provides metrics, logs, and alarms to monitor AWS resources and applications in real-time. CloudWatch is tightly integrated with **AWS Lambda**, allowing you to monitor Lambda functions' performance, behavior, and execution results. It automatically collects standard metrics for Lambda functions, including execution duration, memory usage, and request count.

1. CloudWatch Metrics for AWS Lambda

When you create a Lambda function, AWS CloudWatch automatically collects several key metrics, which can be useful for monitoring the function's performance and identifying any issues.

- **Invocations**: The number of times the Lambda function is invoked.
- **Duration**: The time it takes for the Lambda function to execute, measured in milliseconds.

- **Errors**: The number of failed invocations of the Lambda function (e.g., due to code errors or timeouts).
- **Throttles**: The number of times Lambda was unable to execute the function due to resource limits (e.g., exceeding the concurrency limit).
- **IteratorAge**: For stream-based Lambda triggers (e.g., DynamoDB Streams or Kinesis), the age of the last record processed.

You can view these metrics in the **CloudWatch Console** under **Metrics** > **Lambda**. From there, you can create custom dashboards, monitor trends, and set alarms based on these metrics.

2. Creating a Custom CloudWatch Dashboard

Custom dashboards allow you to visualize the performance of your Lambda functions over time. You can create a dashboard in CloudWatch to track key Lambda metrics such as execution time, errors, and invocations.

Steps to create a custom CloudWatch dashboard:

1. Open the **CloudWatch Console** and select **Dashboards** from the left-hand menu.
2. Click on **Create Dashboard** and give it a name (e.g., LambdaMonitoringDashboard).
3. Choose the type of widget you want to add (e.g., Line, Stack, Number).
4. Select the Lambda metrics you want to display on the dashboard.
5. Save and view the dashboard for real-time monitoring.

This provides a centralized view of your Lambda functions' performance metrics, allowing you to quickly assess their health.

Custom Metrics and Alerts for AWS Lambda

While CloudWatch automatically collects standard metrics for Lambda, you can create **custom metrics** to track specific behaviors or events within your Lambda functions. Additionally, setting up **CloudWatch Alarms** can alert you to potential issues, ensuring you can take action before they affect your application.

1. Creating Custom CloudWatch Metrics

Custom metrics allow you to track application-specific data within your Lambda functions. For instance, if you want to track the number of successful orders processed by a Lambda function, you can send that data to CloudWatch as a custom metric.

Here's an example of how to publish a custom metric from a Lambda function using Python:

python
Copy

```python
import boto3

# Initialize CloudWatch client
cloudwatch = boto3.client('cloudwatch')

def lambda_handler(event, context):
    # Your function logic here (e.g., processing an order)

    # Send custom metric to CloudWatch
    cloudwatch.put_metric_data(
        Namespace='MyAppNamespace',
        MetricData=[
            {
                'MetricName': 'OrdersProcessed',
```

```
    'Dimensions': [
        {
            'Name': 'Region',
            'Value': 'us-west-2'
        },
    ],
    'Value': 1,
    'Unit': 'Count'
    },
  ]
)


return {
    'statusCode': 200,
    'body': 'Order processed and custom metric logged.'
}
```

Explanation:

- **Namespace**: A custom namespace to group related metrics (e.g., MyAppNamespace).
- **MetricName**: The name of the metric (e.g., OrdersProcessed).
- **Dimensions**: Optional metadata that provides additional context for the metric (e.g., Region).
- **Value**: The actual data point you are recording (e.g., 1 for each processed order).
- **Unit**: The unit of measurement (e.g., Count).

You can track multiple custom metrics depending on your application's needs.

2. Creating CloudWatch Alarms for Lambda

Once you have your custom metrics, you can create **CloudWatch Alarms** to monitor these metrics and alert you when certain thresholds are met (e.g., high error rates, timeouts, or unexpected values).

Steps to create a CloudWatch Alarm:

1. Go to the **CloudWatch Console** and select **Alarms** from the left-hand menu.
2. Click **Create Alarm**.
3. Choose a metric (either standard Lambda metrics or your custom metrics).
4. Set the threshold conditions (e.g., if the Errors metric exceeds 5 within 1 minute).
5. Choose the notification actions, such as sending an email or triggering an SNS topic.
6. Save the alarm.

For example, you could set an alarm for **high error rates**:

- If the **Errors** metric for a Lambda function exceeds 5 within 1 minute, trigger an SNS notification to alert the team.

3. Benefits of Custom Metrics and Alarms

- **Proactive Monitoring**: Alarms notify you when something is wrong, allowing you to take action before issues escalate.
- **Granular Visibility**: Custom metrics give you deeper insights into your Lambda functions and application behavior.
- **Real-Time Alerts**: Set up automated alerts through SNS, email, or other services, ensuring that the right team members are notified of issues instantly.

Troubleshooting Lambda Failures with CloudWatch Insights

When things go wrong, **CloudWatch Logs Insights** is a powerful tool for troubleshooting Lambda failures. It allows you to run advanced queries against your logs to identify errors, performance issues, and other anomalies in your Lambda functions.

1. Setting Up CloudWatch Logs for Lambda

By default, AWS Lambda functions log to **CloudWatch Logs**, which you can view and analyze. If you have detailed logging inside your Lambda function, this data will be sent to CloudWatch Logs, where you can use **CloudWatch Logs Insights** to perform advanced queries.

Enable detailed logging in your Lambda function:

- Add custom log statements in your Lambda code using Python's logging module.

python
Copy
```python
import logging

# Set up logging
logger = logging.getLogger()
logger.setLevel(logging.INFO)

def lambda_handler(event, context):
    logger.info("Function started")
```

```
# Your function logic here

logger.info("Function completed")
return {
    'statusCode': 200,
    'body': 'Task completed'
}
```

2. Using CloudWatch Logs Insights for Troubleshooting

Once your Lambda function is logging to CloudWatch, you can use **CloudWatch Logs Insights** to analyze the logs. Insights allows you to run SQL-like queries to extract useful information from the logs.

For example, to identify all **error logs** from your Lambda function, you could use the following query:

```sql
Copy
fields @timestamp, @message
| filter @message like /ERROR/
| sort @timestamp desc
| limit 20
```

This query will return the last 20 log entries that contain the word ERROR. You can customize the query to find specific error patterns, slow execution times, or any other relevant log data.

3. Debugging Lambda Errors with CloudWatch Logs

Here are a few common troubleshooting scenarios and how you can use **CloudWatch Logs Insights** to resolve them:

Timeouts: If your Lambda function is timing out, you can query for logs with long execution times and inspect the logs to see where the function is spending the most time. Example query:

sql

Copy

```
fields @timestamp, @message
| filter @message like /Duration/
| sort @timestamp desc
| limit 50
```

- **Unhandled Exceptions**: Search for unhandled exceptions or error messages in your logs. CloudWatch will capture any errors thrown by the Lambda function. Example query:

  sql

  Copy

  ```
  fields @timestamp, @message
  ```

```
| filter @message like /Exception/
| sort @timestamp desc
| limit 20
```

4. Leveraging CloudWatch Logs Insights for Continuous Improvement

- **Anomaly Detection**: By continuously analyzing Lambda logs, you can detect anomalies in function performance, such as unexpected spikes in execution duration or errors.

- **Root Cause Analysis**: CloudWatch Logs Insights helps you quickly pinpoint the root cause of an issue, reducing the time to resolution.
- **Log Aggregation**: Combine logs from multiple Lambda functions and services to get a comprehensive view of the system's health.

We learned how to manage and monitor AWS Lambda functions using **AWS CloudWatch**. We covered:

- **CloudWatch Metrics**: How to use the built-in metrics and create custom metrics to monitor Lambda performance.
- **CloudWatch Alarms**: How to set up alarms for Lambda functions to get notified about errors, high duration, or other issues.
- **CloudWatch Logs Insights**: How to use CloudWatch Logs and Insights to troubleshoot Lambda failures, monitor logs, and optimize function performance.

By using **CloudWatch** effectively, you can proactively manage your Lambda functions and serverless applications, identify performance bottlenecks, and respond to issues quickly.

Continuous Integration and Deployment for Serverless Apps

We will explore **Continuous Integration and Continuous Deployment (CI/CD)** for serverless applications, focusing on best practices for automating the process of building, testing, and deploying Lambda functions and other serverless resources. We will also discuss **AWS SAM** (Serverless Application Model) and **CloudFormation** for managing and deploying serverless applications efficiently.

Continuous Integration and Deployment for Serverless Apps

Implementing a **CI/CD pipeline** for serverless applications ensures that your code is automatically built, tested, and deployed with minimal manual intervention. This process increases the speed and reliability of deploying updates to serverless applications, which is essential in a fast-paced development environment.

1. Key Concepts in CI/CD for Serverless Applications

A typical CI/CD pipeline for serverless applications follows these steps:

1. **Source Code Management (SCM)**: Use a version control system like **Git** to manage your Lambda functions, API Gateway configurations, and other resources.
2. **Build**: Automatically package and build your Lambda functions and other serverless resources, ensuring they are ready for deployment.
3. **Test**: Run automated tests to ensure that new code changes don't introduce issues. For serverless applications, this may include unit tests for Lambda functions, integration tests, and API tests.
4. **Deploy**: Deploy your serverless application to AWS, automatically creating and updating Lambda functions, API Gateway endpoints, DynamoDB tables, and other resources.
5. **Monitor**: After deployment, monitor the application's performance and errors using **CloudWatch**.

2. Tools for CI/CD with Serverless

Several tools can be used to build a CI/CD pipeline for serverless applications. These tools automate the process of integrating changes, running tests, and deploying to AWS.

- **AWS CodePipeline**: A fully managed CI/CD service that automates the build, test, and deployment processes. It can integrate with other AWS services like CodeBuild, Lambda, and CodeDeploy.

- **AWS CodeBuild**: A fully managed build service that compiles source code, runs tests, and produces build artifacts.
- **Serverless Framework**: A popular open-source framework for building and deploying serverless applications. It provides a set of plugins and tools for deploying Lambda functions and associated resources.
- **GitLab CI/CD / Jenkins / CircleCI**: Third-party CI/CD tools that can integrate with AWS to automate the build and deployment process for serverless applications.

3. Building a CI/CD Pipeline for Serverless Applications

Here's an example of a **CI/CD pipeline** for a Lambda function using **AWS CodePipeline**:

1. **Source Stage**: Set up a source stage to connect your GitHub or CodeCommit repository. This triggers the pipeline whenever code is pushed to a specific branch.
2. **Build Stage**: Use **AWS CodeBuild** to package the Lambda function. You can define build instructions in a buildspec.yml file, which includes steps like installing dependencies, running tests, and packaging the Lambda function code.
3. **Deploy Stage**: Use **AWS CodeDeploy** or **Serverless Framework** to deploy the Lambda function to AWS. The deployment process includes updating the function code, API Gateway, and other resources.
4. **Test Stage**: After deployment, you can run automated tests against the deployed application. These tests can validate Lambda function behavior, API Gateway responses, and DynamoDB operations.
5. **Approval Stage (Optional)**: Before the application is deployed to production, you may want an approval step to ensure manual review.

Managing Serverless Applications with AWS SAM and CloudFormation

Managing the deployment and infrastructure of serverless applications requires an efficient and repeatable process. **AWS SAM** (Serverless Application Model) and **AWS CloudFormation** help manage and deploy serverless resources in a declarative and automated manner.

1. What is AWS SAM (Serverless Application Model)?

AWS SAM is an open-source framework that simplifies the deployment of serverless applications. It extends **AWS CloudFormation** by providing a simplified syntax for defining serverless resources, such as Lambda functions, API Gateway, DynamoDB tables, and S3 buckets.

With SAM, you define your serverless application in a **template.yaml** file, which specifies the configuration for your Lambda functions, API Gateway, and other AWS resources.

2. Example: AWS SAM Template

Here's a simple template.yaml for a serverless application with a Lambda function and an API Gateway endpoint:

yaml

Copy

```
AWSTemplateFormatVersion: '2010-09-09'

Transform: 'AWS::Serverless-2016-10-31'
```

```yaml
Resources:

  MyLambdaFunction:

    Type: 'AWS::Serverless::Function'

    Properties:

      Handler: app.lambda_handler

      Runtime: python3.8

      CodeUri: s3://my-bucket/my-lambda-code.zip

      MemorySize: 128

      Timeout: 10

      Environment:

        Variables:

          MY_ENV_VAR: "value"


  MyApi:

    Type: 'AWS::Serverless::Api'

    Properties:

      StageName: prod

      DefinitionBody:

        swagger: '2.0'
```

```
paths:

/hello:

get:

summary: "Say Hello"

operationId: sayHello

responses:

200:

description: "200 response"
```

Explanation:

- **AWS::Serverless::Function** defines a Lambda function with properties like the handler, runtime, memory size, and environment variables.
- **AWS::Serverless::Api** defines an API Gateway REST API with a /hello path, which maps to the Lambda function.

3. Deploying with AWS SAM CLI

Once you have your template.yaml file, you can use the **AWS SAM CLI** to build, test, and deploy your serverless application.

Steps for deploying with SAM:

1. **Build**: Run sam build to compile your serverless application.
2. **Test Locally**: Run sam local invoke to test Lambda functions locally using Docker.

3. **Deploy**: Use sam deploy to deploy the application to AWS. This will create a CloudFormation stack and deploy all the resources defined in your SAM template.

4. Managing Infrastructure with AWS CloudFormation

AWS CloudFormation is a service that allows you to manage your infrastructure as code. It uses **JSON** or **YAML** templates to describe the AWS resources needed for your application, such as Lambda functions, DynamoDB tables, VPCs, and more.

CloudFormation allows you to provision, update, and manage resources in a repeatable and consistent way.

When you use **SAM**, it automatically creates a **CloudFormation** stack behind the scenes to manage the infrastructure. You can also directly use **CloudFormation** to manage more complex applications or when you need full control over the resources.

5. Benefits of Using SAM and CloudFormation for Serverless

- **Simplified Resource Definitions**: SAM simplifies the process of defining serverless resources like Lambda functions, API Gateway, and DynamoDB with a concise syntax.
- **Infrastructure as Code**: Both SAM and CloudFormation allow you to treat your infrastructure as code, enabling version control and reproducibility.
- **Automated Deployment**: You can automate the deployment process using SAM CLI, AWS CodePipeline, or other CI/CD tools.
- **Version Control**: Manage changes to your infrastructure and applications with CloudFormation templates, providing versioning and rollback capabilities.

Best Practices for CI/CD and Serverless

To ensure successful CI/CD pipelines and efficient management of serverless applications, it's important to follow a few best practices:

1. Use Infrastructure as Code (IaC)

Always define your serverless application infrastructure using **AWS SAM** or **CloudFormation** templates. This practice makes it easier to deploy, manage, and reproduce your serverless environments.

2. Automate Testing

Automate unit tests, integration tests, and end-to-end tests as part of your CI/CD pipeline. This will ensure that your Lambda functions and APIs behave as expected when updates are made.

3. Use AWS CodePipeline for Automated Deployments

Integrate **AWS CodePipeline** with tools like **AWS CodeBuild** and **AWS CodeDeploy** for automated testing and deployment. Set up stages for building, testing, and deploying your Lambda functions to multiple environments (e.g., dev, staging, and production).

4. Monitor and Optimize Lambda Function Performance

Set up **CloudWatch metrics and alarms** for your Lambda functions to monitor performance, identify bottlenecks, and proactively manage failures. Optimize your Lambda functions for cost and performance by adjusting memory, execution time, and request concurrency limits.

5. Use Environment Variables and Secrets Management

Store sensitive information like API keys, database credentials, and configuration values in **AWS Secrets Manager** or **AWS Systems Manager Parameter Store** instead of hardcoding them in your Lambda functions. This practice enhances security and simplifies environment configuration.

In this chapter, we covered **Continuous Integration and Deployment (CI/CD)** best practices for serverless applications using **AWS CodePipeline, AWS SAM**, and **CloudFormation**. We also explored how to manage serverless applications effectively using AWS SAM, which simplifies the deployment process by providing an easy way to define Lambda functions, API Gateway, and other serverless resources. Finally, we discussed the importance of Infrastructure as Code (IaC) for managing serverless applications and the best practices to follow to ensure a reliable, scalable, and maintainable deployment process.

Chapter 13: Continuous Integration and Deployment for Serverless Apps and Managing Serverless Applications with AWS SAM and CloudFormation

In this chapter, we will explore **Continuous Integration and Continuous Deployment (CI/CD)** for serverless applications, focusing on best practices for automating the process of building, testing, and deploying Lambda functions and other serverless resources. We will also discuss **AWS SAM** (Serverless Application Model) and **CloudFormation** for managing and deploying serverless applications efficiently.

Continuous Integration and Deployment for Serverless Apps

Implementing a **CI/CD pipeline** for serverless applications ensures that your code is automatically built, tested, and deployed with minimal manual intervention. This process increases the speed and reliability of deploying updates to serverless applications, which is essential in a fast-paced development environment.

1. Key Concepts in CI/CD for Serverless Applications

A typical CI/CD pipeline for serverless applications follows these steps:

1. **Source Code Management (SCM)**: Use a version control system like **Git** to manage your Lambda functions, API Gateway configurations, and other resources.

2. **Build**: Automatically package and build your Lambda functions and other serverless resources, ensuring they are ready for deployment.

3. **Test**: Run automated tests to ensure that new code changes don't introduce issues. For serverless applications, this may include unit tests for Lambda functions, integration tests, and API tests.
4. **Deploy**: Deploy your serverless application to AWS, automatically creating and updating Lambda functions, API Gateway endpoints, DynamoDB tables, and other resources.
5. **Monitor**: After deployment, monitor the application's performance and errors using **CloudWatch**.

2. Tools for CI/CD with Serverless

Several tools can be used to build a CI/CD pipeline for serverless applications. These tools automate the process of integrating changes, running tests, and deploying to AWS.

- **AWS CodePipeline**: A fully managed CI/CD service that automates the build, test, and deployment processes. It can integrate with other AWS services like CodeBuild, Lambda, and CodeDeploy.
- **AWS CodeBuild**: A fully managed build service that compiles source code, runs tests, and produces build artifacts.
- **Serverless Framework**: A popular open-source framework for building and deploying serverless applications. It provides a set of plugins and tools for deploying Lambda functions and associated resources.
- **GitLab CI/CD / Jenkins / CircleCI**: Third-party CI/CD tools that can integrate with AWS to automate the build and deployment process for serverless applications.

3. Building a CI/CD Pipeline for Serverless Applications

Here's an example of a **CI/CD pipeline** for a Lambda function using **AWS CodePipeline**:

1. **Source Stage**: Set up a source stage to connect your GitHub or CodeCommit repository. This triggers the pipeline whenever code is pushed to a specific branch.
2. **Build Stage**: Use **AWS CodeBuild** to package the Lambda function. You can define build instructions in a buildspec.yml file, which includes steps like installing dependencies, running tests, and packaging the Lambda function code.
3. **Deploy Stage**: Use **AWS CodeDeploy** or **Serverless Framework** to deploy the Lambda function to AWS. The deployment process includes updating the function code, API Gateway, and other resources.
4. **Test Stage**: After deployment, you can run automated tests against the deployed application. These tests can validate Lambda function behavior, API Gateway responses, and DynamoDB operations.
5. **Approval Stage (Optional)**: Before the application is deployed to production, you may want an approval step to ensure manual review.

Managing Serverless Applications with AWS SAM and CloudFormation

Managing the deployment and infrastructure of serverless applications requires an efficient and repeatable process. **AWS SAM** (Serverless Application Model) and **AWS CloudFormation** help manage and deploy serverless resources in a declarative and automated manner.

1. What is AWS SAM (Serverless Application Model)?

AWS SAM is an open-source framework that simplifies the deployment of serverless applications. It extends **AWS CloudFormation** by providing a simplified syntax for defining serverless resources, such as Lambda functions, API Gateway, DynamoDB tables, and S3 buckets.

With SAM, you define your serverless application in a **template.yaml** file, which specifies the configuration for your Lambda functions, API Gateway, and other AWS resources.

2. Example: AWS SAM Template

Here's a simple template.yaml for a serverless application with a Lambda function and an API Gateway endpoint:

yaml
Copy

```yaml
AWSTemplateFormatVersion: '2010-09-09'
Transform: 'AWS::Serverless-2016-10-31'

Resources:
  MyLambdaFunction:
    Type: 'AWS::Serverless::Function'
    Properties:
      Handler: app.lambda_handler
      Runtime: python3.8
      CodeUri: s3://my-bucket/my-lambda-code.zip
      MemorySize: 128
      Timeout: 10
      Environment:
        Variables:
          MY_ENV_VAR: "value"

  MyApi:
    Type: 'AWS::Serverless::Api'
    Properties:
      StageName: prod
```

```
DefinitionBody:
  swagger: '2.0'
  paths:
    /hello:
      get:
        summary: "Say Hello"
        operationId: sayHello
        responses:
          200:
            description: "200 response"
```

Explanation:

- **AWS::Serverless::Function** defines a Lambda function with properties like the handler, runtime, memory size, and environment variables.
- **AWS::Serverless::Api** defines an API Gateway REST API with a /hello path, which maps to the Lambda function.

3. Deploying with AWS SAM CLI

Once you have your template.yaml file, you can use the **AWS SAM CLI** to build, test, and deploy your serverless application.

Steps for deploying with SAM:

1. **Build**: Run sam build to compile your serverless application.
2. **Test Locally**: Run sam local invoke to test Lambda functions locally using Docker.
3. **Deploy**: Use sam deploy to deploy the application to AWS. This will create a CloudFormation stack and deploy all the resources defined in your SAM template.

4. Managing Infrastructure with AWS CloudFormation

AWS CloudFormation is a service that allows you to manage your infrastructure as code. It uses **JSON** or **YAML** templates to describe the AWS resources needed for your application, such as Lambda functions, DynamoDB tables, VPCs, and more.

CloudFormation allows you to provision, update, and manage resources in a repeatable and consistent way.

When you use **SAM**, it automatically creates a **CloudFormation** stack behind the scenes to manage the infrastructure. You can also directly use **CloudFormation** to manage more complex applications or when you need full control over the resources.

5. Benefits of Using SAM and CloudFormation for Serverless

- **Simplified Resource Definitions**: SAM simplifies the process of defining serverless resources like Lambda functions, API Gateway, and DynamoDB with a concise syntax.
- **Infrastructure as Code**: Both SAM and CloudFormation allow you to treat your infrastructure as code, enabling version control and reproducibility.
- **Automated Deployment**: You can automate the deployment process using SAM CLI, AWS CodePipeline, or other CI/CD tools.
- **Version Control**: Manage changes to your infrastructure and applications with CloudFormation templates, providing versioning and rollback capabilities.

Best Practices for CI/CD and Serverless

To ensure successful CI/CD pipelines and efficient management of serverless applications, it's important to follow a few best practices:

199

1. Use Infrastructure as Code (IaC)

Always define your serverless application infrastructure using **AWS SAM** or **CloudFormation** templates. This practice makes it easier to deploy, manage, and reproduce your serverless environments.

2. Automate Testing

Automate unit tests, integration tests, and end-to-end tests as part of your CI/CD pipeline. This will ensure that your Lambda functions and APIs behave as expected when updates are made.

3. Use AWS CodePipeline for Automated Deployments

Integrate **AWS CodePipeline** with tools like **AWS CodeBuild** and **AWS CodeDeploy** for automated testing and deployment. Set up stages for building, testing, and deploying your Lambda functions to multiple environments (e.g., dev, staging, and production).

4. Monitor and Optimize Lambda Function Performance

Set up **CloudWatch metrics and alarms** for your Lambda functions to monitor performance, identify bottlenecks, and proactively manage failures. Optimize your Lambda functions for cost and performance by adjusting memory, execution time, and request concurrency limits.

5. Use Environment Variables and Secrets Management

Store sensitive information like API keys, database credentials, and configuration values in **AWS Secrets Manager** or **AWS Systems Manager Parameter Store** instead of hardcoding them in your Lambda functions. This practice enhances security and simplifies environment configuration.

We covered **Continuous Integration and Deployment (CI/CD)** best practices for serverless applications using **AWS CodePipeline, AWS SAM**, and **CloudFormation**. We also explored how to manage serverless applications effectively using AWS SAM, which simplifies the deployment process by providing an easy way to define Lambda functions, API Gateway, and other serverless resources. Finally, we discussed the importance of Infrastructure as Code (IaC) for managing serverless applications and the best practices to follow to ensure a reliable, scalable, and maintainable deployment process.

Managing Serverless Apps at Scale with AWS Lambda

We will discuss how to manage serverless applications at scale using **AWS Lambda**. Serverless applications are inherently scalable, but understanding how to leverage AWS services for **horizontal scaling**, and how to handle **heavy traffic** and **ensure high availability** is crucial for building production-grade applications. We'll explore best practices and strategies for managing serverless applications as they grow, enabling them to scale seamlessly with demand.

Horizontal Scaling in Serverless Environments

One of the key benefits of **AWS Lambda** is its ability to automatically scale based on the number of requests. **Horizontal scaling** refers to increasing the number of instances of a service in response to increased traffic. With AWS Lambda, this scaling is handled automatically, but understanding how it works and how to configure resources for optimal scaling is important.

1. How AWS Lambda Handles Scaling

AWS Lambda automatically scales to meet demand by creating new instances of the function to handle incoming requests. Each request is processed in isolation, so the function can scale independently based on the number of concurrent executions.

- **Concurrency**: Lambda scales horizontally by increasing the number of concurrent executions, which means multiple instances of the Lambda function run in parallel to handle traffic spikes. Lambda will provision additional execution environments as necessary to handle the load.
- **Reserved Concurrency**: For critical functions that need to scale quickly, you can reserve a specific amount of concurrency, ensuring that Lambda will allocate dedicated resources to those functions, even during high-demand periods.
- **Provisioned Concurrency**: If you require low-latency performance, you can enable **Provisioned Concurrency** for Lambda functions. This feature ensures that a specific number of instances of the function are pre-warmed and ready to handle requests instantly, reducing cold start latency.

2. Setting Up Reserved Concurrency and Provisioned Concurrency

- **Reserved Concurrency**: To ensure that Lambda has the required resources for specific functions, you can reserve a set amount of concurrency. This is particularly useful for functions that need to handle critical workloads that must not be throttled or delayed.
  Steps to enable Reserved Concurrency:
  1. Go to the **Lambda Console**.
  2. Select your Lambda function.
  3. In the **Concurrency** section, set the **Reserved Concurrency** value to the desired number of concurrent executions.
- **Provisioned Concurrency**: To reduce cold start latency and ensure that a Lambda function is always ready to process events, use Provisioned Concurrency. This setting pre-warms Lambda instances, ensuring that they are

202

ready to serve requests immediately.

Steps to enable Provisioned Concurrency:

1. Go to the **Lambda Console** and select your function.
2. Under the **Concurrency** section, choose **Provisioned Concurrency** and set the desired concurrency.
3. Set the target concurrency value, which will be pre-warmed for consistent performance.

Handling Heavy Traffic and High Availability in Serverless

While AWS Lambda is designed to scale automatically, there are additional strategies you can implement to handle **heavy traffic** and ensure **high availability**. These strategies involve a combination of Lambda features, architectural best practices, and integration with other AWS services.

1. Ensuring High Availability with Lambda and AWS Services

To achieve **high availability** in a serverless application, it's important to ensure that Lambda functions and other AWS services are distributed across multiple Availability Zones (AZs) within a region. This minimizes the risk of downtime in case one Availability Zone experiences issues.

- **AWS Lambda Availability**: AWS Lambda functions are automatically distributed across multiple **Availability Zones** in a region. This ensures that even if one AZ becomes unavailable, the Lambda function can still be invoked from other AZs.
- **Cross-Region Replication**: For **global applications**, you can use **AWS Lambda@Edge** in conjunction with **Amazon CloudFront** to run Lambda functions at AWS locations closer to end users, improving performance and availability.

- **Fault Tolerance with SQS and SNS**: For event-driven architectures, using **Amazon SQS** (Simple Queue Service) and **SNS** (Simple Notification Service) can help decouple components and build a fault-tolerant architecture. SQS queues can buffer requests to Lambda functions, allowing the functions to scale independently and process messages as they are available.

2. Handling High Traffic with AWS Lambda and API Gateway

When handling high levels of incoming traffic, **API Gateway** plays a vital role in managing the load and ensuring that the requests are properly routed to Lambda functions. Together with Lambda, API Gateway provides the necessary tools to scale and manage large volumes of traffic efficiently.

- **API Gateway Throttling and Rate Limiting**: You can configure **throttling** and **rate limits** on API Gateway to protect your Lambda functions from being overwhelmed by traffic spikes.
  Steps to configure throttling:
  1. Go to the **API Gateway Console**.
  2. Select your API and navigate to **Stage Settings**.
  3. Set the **Throttle** limits to specify the maximum number of requests per second.
- **Caching**: For read-heavy applications, consider using **API Gateway caching**. Caching responses from Lambda functions reduces the load on your Lambda functions and speeds up response times by returning data from the cache instead of invoking the function for every request.
- **AWS WAF (Web Application Firewall)**: To protect your serverless application from malicious traffic, use **AWS WAF** in front of API Gateway to filter and block harmful requests before they reach your Lambda function.

3. Auto-Scaling Other AWS Services

Lambda is only one part of a serverless application, and many serverless applications rely on other AWS services like **DynamoDB, S3**, and **SNS** to handle various tasks. Ensuring that these services scale properly is essential for maintaining performance during high traffic.

- **Amazon DynamoDB Auto-Scaling**: DynamoDB automatically scales to accommodate increasing traffic, but you can configure **auto-scaling** settings to adjust throughput capacity based on demand. This ensures that DynamoDB can handle large bursts of traffic without manual intervention.
  Steps to enable auto-scaling for DynamoDB:
  1. Go to the **DynamoDB Console**.
  2. Select your table and navigate to **Auto Scaling**.
  3. Set the target utilization and scaling policies to automatically adjust read and write throughput as needed.
- **Amazon S3**: Amazon S3 is highly scalable and can handle large amounts of data. S3 is designed to scale automatically to accommodate high request volumes, so you don't need to worry about scaling this service manually.

Optimizing Performance During High Traffic

As traffic increases, Lambda functions may experience **cold starts** (especially if using **Provisioned Concurrency** is not feasible), leading to longer response times. Here are some strategies for optimizing performance during high traffic:

1. Optimize Lambda Performance

- **Keep Lambda Functions Small**: Smaller Lambda functions reduce initialization time (cold starts) and execution time. Ensure that Lambda functions only include the necessary dependencies.

- **Use Lightweight Libraries**: Instead of using large third-party libraries, opt for lightweight alternatives to reduce the package size and cold start duration.
- **Provisioned Concurrency**: Pre-warming Lambda instances with **Provisioned Concurrency** ensures that you have a set number of pre-initialized Lambda instances ready to handle requests with minimal latency.

2. Use Caching with API Gateway

API Gateway caching can significantly reduce load on your Lambda functions by storing responses for frequent requests. This minimizes the need to invoke Lambda functions for every single request, which is particularly useful for read-heavy workloads.

- **Cache Expiration**: Set cache expiration to balance the trade-off between reducing Lambda invocations and ensuring data freshness.
- **Conditional Caching**: Use caching only for certain HTTP methods (e.g., GET), and bypass the cache for methods like POST, PUT, or DELETE.

3. Avoid Overloading Lambda Functions

Lambda functions have concurrent execution limits that can be affected by the overall load in the region. You can configure **concurrency limits** in Lambda to avoid overloading the service and ensure fair distribution of resources.

- **Use Multiple Lambda Functions**: Split workloads into smaller, modular functions to distribute load effectively. For example, handle heavy data processing in a separate Lambda function that runs in parallel with the main function.

In this chapter, we explored how to manage **serverless applications at scale** with **AWS Lambda**, focusing on key strategies for **horizontal scaling, handling high traffic**, and ensuring **high availability**. We discussed the **automatic scaling** capabilities of Lambda, how to leverage **API Gateway** for traffic management, and the importance of using other AWS services like **DynamoDB** for scalable storage. Additionally, we looked at ways to optimize Lambda performance and ensure your serverless application can handle large traffic spikes efficiently.

Serverless applications offer unparalleled scalability and flexibility, but as they grow, it's essential to implement the right strategies to manage traffic, ensure availability, and optimize performance. By following the practices outlined in this chapter, you can ensure that your serverless applications are robust, scalable, and ready for production.

Chapter 14: Optimizing Serverless Apps for High Availability and Performance

In this chapter, we will explore best practices for **optimizing serverless applications** to ensure **high availability** and **performance**. We will focus on **Lambda performance optimization**, managing **API Gateway** for scalability, and optimizing **data access patterns in DynamoDB**. As your serverless applications grow in size and complexity, these optimizations are critical to ensuring that your application can scale efficiently and handle high traffic while maintaining fast response times.

Best Practices for Lambda Performance Optimization

AWS Lambda offers significant performance benefits for serverless applications, but optimizing its execution is essential for reducing latency, improving throughput, and ensuring cost-efficiency. Lambda optimizations can be categorized into the following areas: **cold start optimization, resource allocation, function size**, and **code optimization**.

1. Reducing Cold Start Latency

Cold starts occur when AWS Lambda needs to initialize a new instance of your function to handle a request. This initialization can introduce latency, especially for larger functions or those with many dependencies. To optimize for cold starts:

- **Use Provisioned Concurrency**: Provisioned Concurrency ensures that a specified number of Lambda instances are always warm and ready to handle requests. This can significantly reduce cold start latency for high-demand functions.

  How to Enable Provisioned Concurrency:

- Go to the **Lambda Console**.
- Select your function.
- In the **Concurrency** section, enable **Provisioned Concurrency** and set the desired number of pre-warmed instances.

- **Reduce Function Size**: Lambda's cold start time increases with the size of the function deployment package. To minimize cold start time:
  - **Trim unused dependencies**: Only include the necessary libraries and dependencies for your function.
  - **Use Lambda Layers**: Move common dependencies (such as large libraries) to Lambda Layers, which can be shared between multiple functions, reducing the size of your deployment package.

- **Choose the Right Memory Allocation**: Memory allocation in Lambda determines both the CPU and memory resources available to your function. Allocating more memory to your Lambda function typically increases its CPU power, reducing execution time for compute-intensive tasks. However, this comes at a higher cost, so balance memory allocation based on your function's needs.

- **Optimize the Language Runtime**: Some programming languages, like Node.js and Python, tend to have faster cold start times compared to others like Java or .NET Core. If cold start latency is a major concern, consider using a lighter runtime like Node.js or Python for functions that are invoked frequently.

2. Lambda Execution Duration and Timeout Settings

The execution time of a Lambda function is one of the primary factors in determining performance. AWS Lambda allows you to set a maximum execution timeout (up to 15 minutes per invocation). Setting the correct timeout is critical to prevent functions from running too long, especially when they're waiting for external services.

- **Set an Appropriate Timeout**: A shorter timeout can reduce costs by ensuring Lambda does not run beyond necessary limits, but ensure that your function has enough time to complete its work. Monitor function execution and adjust the timeout based on actual usage patterns.

- **Leverage Asynchronous Invocations**: If your function handles long-running tasks, consider invoking it asynchronously. This allows your Lambda function to return immediately, passing the heavy lifting to a background process, and frees up resources for other tasks.

3. Optimize Lambda Code and Dependencies

Efficient code is crucial to optimize Lambda function performance. Reducing execution time and memory usage is key for performance optimization.

- **Minimize Initialization Time**: In Lambda, code that runs during initialization (outside of the function handler) contributes to the cold start time. To reduce this, ensure that only essential code runs during initialization and move non-critical operations into the function handler.
- **Leverage Concurrent Execution**: Use multiple invocations of Lambda functions running concurrently to process large datasets in parallel. This can speed up batch processing tasks and reduce overall processing time.
- **Efficient Database Connections**: Opening new database connections within a Lambda function during each invocation can slow down your application. Reuse database connections wherever possible and consider using connection pooling for faster data access.

Managing API Gateway for Performance and Scalability

API Gateway serves as the entry point for HTTP-based requests to your serverless application. To ensure that your API Gateway can handle increasing traffic without degrading performance, you must implement proper optimization and scaling strategies.

1. Enable Caching for API Gateway

Caching responses in **API Gateway** can dramatically reduce the load on Lambda functions by returning cached data for frequently requested resources.

- **Cache Responses**: Enable response caching in API Gateway to store the result of function invocations. This helps reduce the number of calls to Lambda functions, especially for read-heavy workloads, improving response times.
  Steps to enable caching in API Gateway:
    1. Go to the **API Gateway Console**.
    2. Select the API and choose the **Stage** you want to enable caching for.
    3. Under the **Cache Settings**, enable **Cache** and configure the time-to-live (TTL) for caching responses.
- **Set Appropriate TTL (Time-to-Live)**: Cache invalidation and expiry times are important. Too short of a TTL can increase the number of Lambda function calls, while too long can result in stale data being served.

2. Use Rate Limiting and Throttling

To prevent API Gateway from being overwhelmed during traffic spikes, configure **rate limiting** and **throttling**.

- **Rate Limiting**: Set up a **usage plan** in API Gateway to limit the number of requests per second for specific clients. This helps protect your backend Lambda functions from being overloaded.
  How to configure usage plans:
    1. Go to the **API Gateway Console**.
    2. Select **Usage Plans** and create a new usage plan.
    3. Set rate limits (e.g., 1000 requests per second) and quota limits for different users.

- **Throttling**: Set a **throttle limit** at the API Gateway stage level. This ensures that excessive requests from a single source won't overwhelm your Lambda functions.

3. Use Lambda Authorizers for Fine-Grained Access Control

To scale your serverless application securely, use **Lambda authorizers** in API Gateway for authentication and authorization. This allows you to customize authentication logic, such as validating JWT tokens or checking user permissions before invoking your Lambda functions.

4. Use HTTP APIs for Lower Latency

If your application does not require advanced features like custom authorizers, API Gateway **HTTP APIs** can provide lower latency and better cost-efficiency than the standard **REST APIs**.

- **HTTP APIs** are designed for simpler use cases and provide native support for Lambda integration, reduced overhead, and better performance.

Optimizing Data Access Patterns in DynamoDB

DynamoDB is a fully managed NoSQL database that provides high performance at any scale. However, for optimal performance, it's crucial to understand **how to structure data**, **optimize queries**, and **manage indexing** for your serverless application.

1. Choosing the Right Data Model

Choosing the correct data model is essential for ensuring that DynamoDB scales efficiently and supports your access patterns.

- **Primary Keys**: Design your partition key and sort key to support your most frequent queries. DynamoDB performs best when you query data using the primary key or a **secondary index**.
- **Global Secondary Indexes (GSI)**: GSIs allow you to query DynamoDB based on non-primary key attributes. Use GSIs to support additional query patterns, but avoid over-indexing, as it can increase write costs.
- **Denormalization**: DynamoDB is optimized for simple lookups, so it's best to use **denormalization** (storing multiple copies of data in different places) to reduce the need for joins. This can result in faster queries and reduced complexity.

2. Efficient Querying and Scan Operations

- **Query**: Always use the **Query** operation instead of **Scan** when possible. Scans are costly because they examine all items in a table, while queries only retrieve items based on primary keys or indexed attributes.
- **Pagination**: When querying large datasets, use **pagination** to limit the number of results returned in a single call. This prevents your Lambda functions from being overwhelmed with too much data.

3. Provisioned vs. On-Demand Capacity

DynamoDB offers two capacity modes: **Provisioned** and **On-Demand**.

- **Provisioned**: In **Provisioned** mode, you set the read and write capacity units (RCUs and WCUs). This is ideal when your workload has predictable traffic patterns.
- **On-Demand**: In **On-Demand** mode, DynamoDB automatically scales based on your workload, which is perfect for unpredictable or variable workloads. However, On-Demand mode can be more expensive at high traffic levels, so use it carefully for workloads with inconsistent access patterns.

4. Using DynamoDB Streams for Real-Time Processing

For real-time data processing, use **DynamoDB Streams** to capture changes in your DynamoDB tables. Streams allow you to trigger AWS Lambda functions when items are added, modified, or deleted, enabling real-time workflows like order processing or notifications.

We covered key strategies for **optimizing serverless applications** for **high availability** and **performance**. We focused on best practices for:

- **Lambda performance optimization**: Reducing cold start latency, optimizing function size, and efficiently allocating resources.
- **Managing API Gateway for performance and scalability**: Enabling caching, rate limiting, and throttling to improve the performance and reliability of your serverless APIs.
- **Optimizing data access patterns in DynamoDB**: Designing the right data model, using efficient queries, and leveraging DynamoDB Streams for real-time data processing.

These optimizations will help you build serverless applications that can handle high traffic, scale seamlessly, and deliver fast performance. In the next chapter, we will discuss **security best practices** for serverless applications, focusing on securing Lambda functions, API Gateway, and managing access to sensitive data.

Caching Strategies for Serverless Applications and Using Amazon S3 for Scalable Storage

We will discuss **caching strategies** for serverless applications and explore how **Amazon S3** can be used for scalable, cost-efficient storage. Caching and storage optimization are essential for improving the performance and cost-effectiveness of serverless applications, particularly when dealing with high traffic, large datasets, or frequently accessed resources.

Caching Strategies for Serverless Applications

Caching is a technique used to store frequently accessed data temporarily in a storage layer that is faster to access than the original data source. Caching reduces latency, minimizes calls to backend services (like AWS Lambda or DynamoDB), and can significantly reduce costs by preventing unnecessary invocations of serverless functions.

1. Why Caching is Important in Serverless Applications

Serverless applications, by nature, often rely on services like **AWS Lambda** for computing and **Amazon DynamoDB** for data storage. While these services scale automatically, frequently accessing them can introduce latency and increase costs. Caching helps mitigate these challenges by providing fast access to commonly used data, reducing load on backend systems, and improving response times.

2. Types of Caching in Serverless Architectures

There are several caching strategies you can implement in serverless applications, each suited to different use cases:

- **Lambda Function Result Caching**: Cache the results of Lambda function invocations for commonly requested data. For example, if a Lambda function fetches data from DynamoDB that doesn't change frequently, you can cache the result in **API Gateway** or an external caching service like **Amazon ElastiCache**.

- **API Gateway Caching**: API Gateway supports built-in caching for responses returned by Lambda functions. This reduces the number of requests that reach Lambda, improving performance and reducing costs.
- **Distributed Caching with Amazon ElastiCache**: Amazon ElastiCache offers managed caching for frequently accessed data. It supports **Redis** and **Memcached**, both of which are fast, in-memory data stores used to cache data and reduce load on databases and Lambda functions.

3. API Gateway Caching

API Gateway provides caching capabilities that help reduce the load on backend Lambda functions by caching responses for a configurable time period (TTL – Time to Live). This is particularly useful when responses don't change frequently, such as data that doesn't need to be dynamically recalculated every time.

How to Enable Caching in API Gateway:

1. Go to the **API Gateway Console**.
2. Select your API and go to the **Stages** section.
3. Choose the stage (e.g., prod) and then click on the **Cache Settings**.
4. Enable **Cache** and set the TTL (Time-to-Live) to determine how long the cached data should remain valid.
5. Optionally, enable **Cache Encryption** to encrypt cached responses for additional security.

This will ensure that subsequent requests for the same data are served from the cache instead of invoking the Lambda function, thereby improving performance and reducing costs.

4. Using Amazon ElastiCache for Distributed Caching

For more advanced caching needs, particularly when managing large volumes of data or complex application architectures, **Amazon ElastiCache** provides a distributed caching solution. ElastiCache supports both **Redis** and **Memcached**, offering high-performance, in-memory data stores.

Common Use Cases for ElastiCache:

- **Caching Query Results**: Store the results of frequent database queries to reduce the load on **DynamoDB** or **RDS**.
- **Session Management**: Use Redis for managing user sessions across multiple Lambda invocations.
- **Stateful Applications**: Use Redis to maintain the state in stateless serverless applications that require shared memory across different invocations.

Steps to Set Up ElastiCache:

1. Go to the **ElastiCache Console**.
2. Choose either **Redis** or **Memcached**, depending on your use case.
3. Create a new cluster and configure the desired settings (e.g., node type, replication).
4. Connect your Lambda functions to ElastiCache using the appropriate AWS SDK (boto3 for Python).
5. Use ElastiCache to store frequently accessed data or application states.

Example of Using Redis with Lambda:

python
Copy

```
import redis
import os
```

```
# Connect to Redis
redis_host = os.environ['REDIS_HOST']
redis_port = os.environ['REDIS_PORT']
cache = redis.StrictRedis(host=redis_host, port=redis_port, db=0)

def lambda_handler(event, context):
    # Check if data is in cache
    cached_data = cache.get('user_data')

    if cached_data:
        return {
            'statusCode': 200,
            'body': f'Cached data: {cached_data}'
        }

    # If not in cache, fetch data from the source
    user_data = fetch_user_data_from_db()

    # Cache the data for future use
    cache.set('user_data', user_data, ex=60)  # Expire in 60 seconds

    return {
        'statusCode': 200,
        'body': f'Fetched data: {user_data}'
    }
```

In the above example, we use **Redis** to cache user data for 60 seconds. If the data is already cached, it is returned immediately; otherwise, it is fetched from the database and then cached for future use.

5. Best Practices for Caching in Serverless

- **Set Appropriate TTL**: Choose an appropriate TTL to balance between reducing calls to backend services and ensuring data freshness.
- **Cache Invalidations**: Implement a mechanism to invalidate or refresh cached data when the underlying data changes, ensuring that the cache always contains valid data.
- **Use Caching for Expensive Operations**: Cache the results of expensive or time-consuming operations, such as API calls, database queries, or data processing tasks.

Using Amazon S3 for Scalable Storage

Amazon S3 is a highly durable, scalable, and cost-effective object storage service that can be used to store large amounts of data, such as images, videos, backups, and log files. S3 integrates seamlessly with AWS Lambda and can be used to trigger Lambda functions when new data is uploaded, allowing you to build scalable workflows.

1. Why Use Amazon S3 in Serverless Applications?

Amazon S3 offers several benefits for serverless applications:

- **Scalability**: S3 automatically scales to store and retrieve any amount of data without requiring manual intervention.
- **Durability**: S3 provides 99.999999999% (11 9's) durability, making it one of the most reliable storage services available.
- **Cost-Effective**: S3 offers a pay-as-you-go pricing model, ensuring that you only pay for what you use, making it ideal for handling unpredictable workloads.

2. Using S3 with Lambda for Event-Driven Architectures

Amazon S3 can trigger **AWS Lambda** functions in response to various events, such as when an object is uploaded, deleted, or modified. This makes S3 a powerful tool for building event-driven workflows in serverless applications.

Common Use Cases:

- **File Upload and Processing**: Trigger Lambda functions to process files when they are uploaded to S3, such as image resizing, video transcoding, or log file processing.
- **Backup and Storage**: Use Lambda to manage backup processes, where Lambda functions monitor S3 for changes and manage the backup lifecycle.
- **Data Aggregation**: Lambda can aggregate data stored in S3 and send it to other services, such as DynamoDB or Amazon Redshift, for further processing.

3. Example: Processing Files in S3 with Lambda

Suppose you have an application that uploads images to S3, and you need to automatically resize the image when it's uploaded. You can set up an event-driven workflow to trigger a Lambda function.

Lambda Function Example:

python
Copy
```python
import boto3
from PIL import Image
import io

# Initialize S3 client
s3 = boto3.client('s3')
```

```python
def lambda_handler(event, context):
    # Extract the bucket and file name from the event
    bucket_name = event['Records'][0]['s3']['bucket']['name']
    file_name = event['Records'][0]['s3']['object']['key']

    # Download the image from S3
    image_object = s3.get_object(Bucket=bucket_name, Key=file_name)
    image_data = image_object['Body'].read()

    # Process the image (e.g., resize)
    image = Image.open(io.BytesIO(image_data))
    image = image.resize((100, 100))  # Resize the image

    # Save the resized image back to S3
    buffer = io.BytesIO()
    image.save(buffer, 'JPEG')
    buffer.seek(0)
    s3.put_object(Bucket=bucket_name, Key=f"resized/{file_name}", Body=buffer)

    return {
        'statusCode': 200,
        'body': f"Image {file_name} resized and saved."
    }
```

In this example:

- **Lambda** is triggered when an image is uploaded to S3.
- The image is resized and saved back to S3 in a different folder (resized/).

4. Best Practices for Using Amazon S3

- **Use Multipart Upload for Large Files**: When dealing with large files, use S3's **Multipart Upload** feature to upload files in parts, improving performance and reliability.
- **Set Lifecycle Policies**: Use S3's lifecycle policies to automatically transition older data to cheaper storage tiers, such as **S3 Glacier**, or delete old data to optimize storage costs.
- **Implement Data Encryption**: Use **S3 Encryption** to secure sensitive data at rest. You can encrypt objects with **SSE-S3, SSE-KMS, or SSE-C**.

We explored **caching strategies** and **using Amazon S3 for scalable storage** in serverless applications. We covered:

- **Caching with API Gateway, Lambda, and ElastiCache** to improve performance and reduce latency in serverless applications.
- **Amazon S3** as a scalable and cost-effective storage solution, and how it integrates with Lambda to trigger event-driven workflows.
- **Best practices** for implementing caching and optimizing S3 usage for serverless applications.

By using these strategies, you can enhance the performance, scalability, and efficiency of your serverless applications.

Chapter 15: Future of Serverless Applications and Python

In this final chapter, we will look at the **future of serverless applications** and how **Python** continues to evolve within the context of serverless computing. We'll explore **emerging trends** in serverless technology, the growing ecosystem around serverless applications, and how Python is adapting to meet the demands of modern serverless architectures.

Emerging Trends in Serverless Computing

Serverless computing has seen rapid growth in recent years, driven by the benefits of reduced operational complexity, automatic scaling, and cost-efficiency. As more companies adopt serverless architectures, several emerging trends are shaping the future of serverless computing. These trends focus on enhancing performance, addressing limitations, and expanding the use cases for serverless applications.

1. Expansion Beyond Lambda Functions

While AWS Lambda has been the dominant service in the serverless ecosystem, the future of serverless computing is moving beyond Lambda to include **event-driven workflows** and integration with other AWS services, such as **Step Functions**, **AppSync**, and **Fargate**.

- **Event-Driven Architectures**: Event-driven computing is expected to become even more prominent. More serverless services are incorporating event-driven features, making it easier to connect services like Lambda, API Gateway, and Step Functions to orchestrate complex workflows. This makes serverless applications more dynamic and adaptable to changing business requirements.

223

- **Container-based Serverless**: While AWS Lambda has long supported serverless functions, we're seeing a trend toward containerized workloads in the form of **AWS Fargate**. Fargate allows users to run containers without managing servers, providing a serverless experience while still offering the flexibility of containerized applications.
- **Serverless Data Processing**: Services like **AWS Kinesis** and **Amazon Redshift Spectrum** allow serverless data processing at scale, supporting complex analytics and data processing workflows. These services abstract away the infrastructure management, enabling developers to focus on data processing tasks instead of managing clusters.

2. Serverless Frameworks and Tooling

As serverless architectures become more popular, **serverless frameworks** like **Serverless Framework, AWS SAM**, and **Terraform** are evolving to simplify the development and deployment of serverless applications.

- **Unified Deployment and Infrastructure as Code (IaC)**: Serverless frameworks are increasingly supporting IaC practices, allowing developers to define, deploy, and manage their serverless applications in a unified way. These frameworks help automate the deployment of not just functions but also other resources like databases, queues, and event sources.
- **Multi-Cloud Serverless**: Serverless computing was initially dominated by AWS Lambda, but now other cloud providers like **Google Cloud Functions, Azure Functions**, and **IBM Cloud Functions** are gaining traction. Serverless applications are increasingly becoming multi-cloud, and cross-cloud frameworks and tools are emerging to support such architectures.
- **Observability and Monitoring**: Monitoring serverless applications presents a challenge, and as such, tools for observability are becoming a focus. Services like **AWS X-Ray, CloudWatch**, and third-party tools such as **Datadog** and **New**

Relic are evolving to provide deeper insights into serverless applications, helping developers identify performance bottlenecks and optimize resource usage.

3. Serverless Databases and Storage Services

One of the biggest hurdles for serverless applications has been managing databases and state. However, cloud providers are rapidly addressing this with **serverless databases** and **scalable storage services**.

- **Serverless Databases**: Databases like **Amazon Aurora Serverless** and **Amazon DynamoDB** are growing in popularity as serverless storage solutions. These databases automatically scale based on demand, and provide cost-effective storage without the need to manage servers or clusters.
- **Serverless File Storage**: Services like **Amazon S3** have been key players in serverless file storage. The future of serverless computing will see tighter integration between file storage and compute resources, streamlining workflows for applications that involve large datasets, like AI/ML models, IoT, and media processing.

How Python's Ecosystem is Evolving for Serverless

Python has long been a popular language for serverless development due to its simplicity, efficiency, and strong ecosystem. As serverless computing becomes more widespread, Python's ecosystem continues to evolve to support the growing demands of serverless architecture. Here are some key ways Python's ecosystem is adapting to meet the needs of serverless applications.

1. Native Integration with AWS Lambda

Python has become one of the most popular languages for writing AWS Lambda functions, and AWS continues to enhance Python's support in Lambda by improving runtime performance, security features, and developer tools.

- **Lambda Runtime for Python**: AWS Lambda offers an optimized Python runtime that supports the latest versions of Python (e.g., Python 3.8, 3.9). The serverless ecosystem is also moving toward faster startup times, which will further reduce Lambda cold start latency for Python functions.
- **Python Libraries for Serverless**: The Python ecosystem continues to grow, with numerous libraries that simplify serverless development. Libraries like **Zappa, Serverless Framework** for Python, and **AWS SAM CLI** provide easy deployment and management of serverless applications.

2. Serverless Python Frameworks

There is a growing number of frameworks and tools for managing serverless Python applications. These frameworks simplify the development, testing, and deployment of Lambda functions and other serverless resources.

- **Zappa**: Zappa is a Python framework that simplifies the process of deploying Python applications to AWS Lambda and API Gateway. Zappa supports the deployment of **Flask** and **Django** apps to Lambda, making it easier to integrate Python web applications with the serverless model.
- **Serverless Framework**: The **Serverless Framework** provides first-class support for Python, allowing developers to define functions, events, and resources in a simple YAML configuration file. It abstracts away much of the complexity involved in setting up serverless infrastructure, allowing developers to focus on writing business logic.
- **AWS Chalice**: **AWS Chalice** is another Python-specific framework for building serverless applications on AWS. Chalice simplifies the creation of REST APIs,

event-driven Lambda functions, and S3 integrations, enabling developers to easily build scalable, serverless Python applications.

3. Enhanced Support for Data Science and Machine Learning

Python is widely used for **data science**, **machine learning**, and **AI development**, and serverless platforms are increasingly integrating with Python's powerful libraries, such as **TensorFlow**, **PyTorch**, **Scikit-learn**, and **Pandas**. Here's how Python is evolving in the serverless ecosystem for AI/ML use cases:

- **Serverless ML Inference**: Serverless computing is well-suited for machine learning inference, and AWS Lambda now supports the deployment of **machine learning models** directly to Lambda functions. Developers can use Python to build and deploy models on AWS Lambda, benefiting from automatic scaling and reduced operational overhead.

- **Python and AWS SageMaker**: **Amazon SageMaker** has made it easier for developers to run Python-based machine learning workflows in a serverless environment. SageMaker now supports Python-based Jupyter notebooks, allowing developers to train, test, and deploy models without worrying about managing infrastructure.

4. Improved Serverless Python Development Tools

As serverless applications become more complex, the need for effective **local development** and **debugging tools** grows. Python's ecosystem is responding with tools that make it easier to develop, test, and deploy serverless Python applications.

- **Local Development with AWS SAM CLI**: The **AWS SAM CLI** allows developers to run Lambda functions locally on their machines, simulating AWS environments. SAM also supports Python functions, helping developers test and debug serverless functions locally before deploying them to AWS.

- **Mocking AWS Services**: Tools like **localstack** allow developers to mock AWS services locally in Python, which can be invaluable for testing serverless applications without incurring costs or requiring AWS resources during development.

5. Serverless Python and Edge Computing

With the rise of **Lambda@Edge**, Python is increasingly being used for serverless functions that execute closer to users, at the edge of AWS's global network. Lambda@Edge allows Python developers to build **low-latency, scalable applications** that run in response to CloudFront events, making it ideal for content delivery, real-time data processing, and other edge computing use cases.

The future of serverless applications is rapidly evolving, with serverless computing continuing to expand beyond traditional use cases and integrate more deeply with other services and cloud platforms. Python's ecosystem has been a key part of this evolution, offering powerful tools and libraries that make it easier for developers to build, deploy, and scale serverless applications.

We have explored:

- **Emerging trends in serverless computing**, including event-driven architectures, containerized serverless computing, and serverless data processing.
- **How Python is evolving** within the serverless space, with improvements to Lambda support, the rise of Python-based frameworks like Zappa and Chalice, and enhanced integration with machine learning and data science workflows.
- **The role of serverless Python applications** in future architectures, particularly in edge computing, AI/ML, and data processing.

As serverless computing continues to mature, Python's ecosystem will continue to play a pivotal role in shaping the future of cloud-native development. Serverless architectures powered by Python will remain a powerful tool for developers looking to build scalable, cost-effective, and highly performant applications without the overhead of managing infrastructure.

Serverless Technologies Beyond AWS (Azure, Google Cloud, etc.)

We will explore **serverless technologies** beyond **AWS**, such as **Microsoft Azure** and **Google Cloud**, and discuss how these cloud providers are approaching serverless computing. We will also look at the **future of serverless in microservices** and **cloud-native applications**, and provide **next steps** for developers who want to expand their knowledge in the serverless space.

Serverless Technologies Beyond AWS (Azure, Google Cloud, etc.)

While **AWS Lambda** is the most well-known serverless platform, other major cloud providers like **Microsoft Azure**, **Google Cloud**, and **IBM Cloud** have their own serverless offerings. These alternatives offer unique features and integrations, expanding the options available for developers when building serverless applications.

1. Microsoft Azure Serverless Computing

Azure Functions is Microsoft's serverless offering, providing a platform for building event-driven applications. Much like AWS Lambda, Azure Functions allows you to run code in response to various triggers, including HTTP requests, database changes, and message queues.

- **Azure Functions Overview**: Azure Functions supports multiple programming languages, including Python, C#, Java, and JavaScript, making it highly versatile. It also supports **event-driven architectures**, where functions are triggered by events like **HTTP requests, storage changes**, or **message queues**.

- **Integration with Azure Ecosystem**: Azure Functions integrates seamlessly with other Azure services, such as **Azure Event Grid**, **Azure Logic Apps**, and **Azure Storage**, allowing developers to build end-to-end serverless workflows.

Key Features of Azure Functions:

- **Elastic Scaling**: Azure Functions automatically scales based on demand. It can scale from zero to thousands of instances without manual intervention.
- **Consumption and Premium Plans**: Azure offers a **Consumption Plan**, which charges based on usage (similar to AWS Lambda), and a **Premium Plan** that offers more features, such as **VNET integration, custom domains**, and **dedicated compute resources**.

2. Google Cloud Serverless Computing

Google Cloud Functions is Google's serverless computing offering, which allows developers to run event-driven code in response to cloud events. Google Cloud Functions is tightly integrated with Google Cloud's ecosystem, including services like **Google Cloud Pub/Sub**, **Cloud Storage**, and **Firestore**.

- **Google Cloud Functions Overview**: Google Cloud Functions allows you to write code that responds to HTTP triggers or event-based triggers from other Google Cloud services.
- **Serverless Events**: Functions can be triggered by various Google Cloud services, including **Cloud Storage** (e.g., when a file is uploaded), **Cloud Pub/Sub** (e.g., for messaging queues), and **Firestore** (e.g., for document changes).
- **Lightweight Functions**: Google Cloud Functions is optimized for lightweight functions with low latency, making it ideal for real-time applications such as API backends and webhooks.

Key Features of Google Cloud Functions:

- **Seamless Integration with Google Cloud**: Functions are easy to trigger from other Google Cloud services, simplifying the development of serverless applications.
- **Event-Driven Architecture**: Google Cloud Functions is designed to handle events, such as **file uploads, database changes**, or **pub/sub messages**, making it a great fit for microservices and real-time applications.
- **Pricing**: Google Cloud Functions also follows a **pay-as-you-go** pricing model, charging based on the number of invocations, execution time, and allocated memory.

3. IBM Cloud Functions

IBM Cloud Functions is based on **Apache OpenWhisk**, an open-source serverless computing framework. IBM Cloud Functions allows you to run event-driven functions written in multiple languages, including Python, JavaScript, and Java.

- **IBM Cloud Functions Overview**: IBM Cloud Functions enables developers to write functions that run in response to events such as HTTP requests, changes to cloud storage, or messages in queues. It also integrates with other IBM Cloud services, such as **IBM Cloud Object Storage** and **IBM Cloud Databases**.

Key Features of IBM Cloud Functions:

- **Event-Driven**: Functions can be triggered by a wide variety of events from IBM Cloud services, third-party APIs, or custom triggers.
- **Flexible Resource Management**: IBM Cloud Functions allows you to control the memory and execution time of your functions, which is useful for optimizing performance and cost.
- **Open Source**: Being based on Apache OpenWhisk, IBM Cloud Functions is an open-source project that can be used on other cloud platforms or on-premises.

The Future of Serverless in Microservices and Cloud-Native Apps

Serverless computing is playing an increasingly important role in **microservices** and **cloud-native applications**. As businesses move toward microservices architectures and cloud-native development, serverless provides the scalability, flexibility, and cost-efficiency that these architectures require.

1. Serverless and Microservices

Microservices architectures are becoming more popular because they allow for the decoupling of applications into independent, self-contained services. Serverless technologies are a natural fit for microservices, as they allow developers to create small, independently deployable functions that can be triggered by events.

- **Scalability**: Serverless computing automatically scales individual microservices, ensuring that each service can handle the load independently, without the need for manual intervention.

- **Event-Driven Architectures**: Serverless functions work well with event-driven architectures, which are commonly used in microservices. Services can communicate through events (e.g., HTTP requests, messages, or database changes), triggering the appropriate Lambda function or equivalent in other cloud providers.

- **Cost Efficiency**: Serverless microservices enable a pay-as-you-go model, where you only pay for what you use, making it easier to manage costs in a microservices architecture.

2. Cloud-Native Applications and Serverless

Cloud-native applications are designed to run on cloud platforms, making full use of cloud services like **compute, storage, networking**, and **monitoring**. Serverless computing aligns perfectly with cloud-native principles because it abstracts infrastructure management, allowing developers to focus solely on building features.

- **Microservice Evolution**: As more companies adopt microservices, serverless technologies provide the perfect backend for handling each service. Serverless applications fit the cloud-native design by leveraging **statelessness** and **event-driven architectures**.
- **Integration with Cloud-Native Tools**: Serverless functions integrate seamlessly with cloud-native tools like **CI/CD pipelines, Kubernetes, containers**, and **observability platforms** like **Prometheus** and **Grafana**.

3. Multi-Cloud and Hybrid Cloud Architectures

With the rise of multi-cloud strategies, where businesses deploy applications across multiple cloud providers to avoid vendor lock-in, serverless computing offers significant flexibility. Serverless functions are often designed to be platform-agnostic, which is ideal for multi-cloud architectures.

- **Cross-Cloud Serverless**: As multi-cloud adoption increases, serverless functions are expected to become more cross-cloud compatible. Frameworks like **Kubeless** and **Knative** (on Kubernetes) are emerging to support running serverless workloads across different cloud providers, enabling a unified experience across AWS, Azure, Google Cloud, and others.

Next Steps for Developers: Expanding Your Knowledge

As serverless computing continues to evolve, staying up-to-date with new technologies and best practices is essential. Here are some next steps for developers who want to deepen their knowledge of serverless architectures and continue building effective, scalable serverless applications.

1. Learn More About Multi-Cloud and Hybrid Cloud Architectures

As serverless adoption grows, multi-cloud and hybrid cloud deployments will become more common. Understanding how to work with serverless across multiple cloud providers, and integrating cloud-native services with serverless architectures, will be valuable skills.

- **Explore Multi-Cloud Frameworks**: Learn about frameworks like **Kubeless** and **Knative,** which allow serverless functions to run across multiple cloud platforms.
- **Hybrid Cloud Strategies**: Investigate hybrid cloud solutions that combine on-premise infrastructure with serverless computing to meet security and regulatory requirements.

2. Dive Deeper into Serverless Best Practices

To develop production-grade serverless applications, developers need to follow best practices related to performance, security, monitoring, and testing. Understanding these practices will ensure that your serverless applications are scalable, cost-efficient, and reliable.

- **Performance Optimization**: Master techniques for optimizing serverless applications, such as reducing cold start latency, optimizing function size, and fine-tuning API Gateway.

234

- **Security Practices**: Learn how to secure serverless applications, including proper use of IAM roles, encryption, and vulnerability scanning.

3. Stay Current with New Serverless Frameworks and Tools

Serverless frameworks and tools are constantly evolving. Staying up-to-date with the latest features of popular frameworks like **Serverless Framework, AWS SAM, Azure Functions**, and **Google Cloud Functions** will ensure you're using the most efficient tools available.

- **Serverless Framework**: Dive deeper into the **Serverless Framework** to manage serverless applications and deployments. Learn about its plugins and integrations with other tools like **CI/CD**.
- **AWS SAM**: Explore more advanced **AWS SAM** features for managing serverless applications, such as managing local development environments and working with AWS Step Functions.

4. Experiment with Serverless ML and AI

Serverless computing is increasingly being used for **machine learning (ML)** and **artificial intelligence (AI)**. By using serverless functions for real-time data processing and inference, developers can integrate advanced data science models into their applications without worrying about infrastructure management.

- **Explore AWS Lambda with SageMaker**: Learn how to deploy machine learning models using **AWS SageMaker** and invoke them via **AWS Lambda** for scalable, serverless ML applications.
- **Use Serverless Frameworks for AI**: Investigate how frameworks like **TensorFlow** and **PyTorch** are being integrated into serverless workflows for AI-powered applications.

We explored **serverless technologies beyond AWS**, including **Azure Functions** and **Google Cloud Functions**, and discussed the future of serverless in **microservices** and **cloud-native applications**. We also provided **next steps for developers** who want to expand their knowledge in serverless computing, from learning about multi-cloud architectures to diving deeper into serverless best practices and machine learning.

Serverless computing is continuing to evolve, and Python remains one of the best languages to use in building serverless applications. By embracing emerging trends and continuously improving your skills, you can stay ahead of the curve and continue to build scalable, cost-effective, and high-performance serverless applications for the future.

Chapter 16: Conclusion

In this final chapter, we'll wrap up everything you've learned in this book and provide some final words of encouragement as you continue your journey with serverless computing and Python. Serverless architectures are transforming the way applications are built, deployed, and scaled, and Python is a powerful tool in that space. Let's take a moment to reflect on the key takeaways and how you can continue to build and optimize serverless applications.

Recap of What You've Learned

Throughout this book, we've covered a wide range of concepts and practical techniques that are essential for building, managing, and optimizing serverless applications. Here's a quick recap of the main topics we explored:

1. Introduction to Serverless Computing

- **What serverless computing is**: We defined serverless computing as an architecture where developers focus on writing code without worrying about the underlying infrastructure. Cloud providers, like AWS, manage the compute resources, automatically scaling and charging based on usage.
- **Benefits of serverless**: We highlighted how serverless computing enables faster development, reduces operational overhead, and allows businesses to pay only for the resources used, offering scalability, cost efficiency, and flexibility.

2. Python for Serverless Applications

- **Why Python is a great choice for serverless**: Python's simplicity, readability, and extensive ecosystem make it an ideal choice for serverless development. We also explored how Python's libraries and frameworks support serverless use cases.

- **Integrating Python with AWS Lambda**: We discussed how to write Python-based Lambda functions, how to connect them with AWS services, and how to handle event-driven architectures.

3. Setting Up Your Environment and Building Your First Lambda Function

- **Setting up AWS and Python environments**: You learned how to set up AWS CLI, configure IAM roles, and create your first Lambda function, allowing you to test and deploy Python code in a serverless environment.
- **Hands-on examples**: You worked through practical examples of building and deploying serverless applications, from simple functions to more complex workflows using services like API Gateway and DynamoDB.

4. Deep Dive into Lambda and Best Practices for Performance Optimization

- **Lambda architecture and features**: We discussed the core features of AWS Lambda, such as how it scales automatically and the key considerations for optimizing Lambda functions, like memory allocation, reducing cold start latency, and managing execution time.
- **Best practices for optimizing performance**: You learned how to make serverless applications more efficient by optimizing Lambda code, using **Provisioned Concurrency**, and integrating caching strategies with API Gateway.

5. Managing and Monitoring Serverless Applications

- **Using AWS CloudWatch**: We covered how to use AWS CloudWatch for monitoring Lambda functions, creating custom metrics, setting up alerts, and troubleshooting Lambda failures.

- **Debugging and optimizing**: You learned about advanced debugging techniques with CloudWatch Logs Insights, error handling strategies, and how to fine-tune your serverless applications for better performance.

6. Real-World Projects

- **Building a Todo List App**: You walked through the process of building a serverless **Todo List app**, learning how to integrate AWS services like API Gateway, Lambda, and DynamoDB to handle CRUD operations.
- **Creating a Chatbot with AWS Lex**: Another project focused on building a serverless chatbot with AWS Lex and Lambda, which helped you explore AI/ML integrations in serverless applications.

7. Security, Cost Management, and Serverless Optimization

- **Security**: You gained an understanding of how to secure your Lambda functions using IAM roles and policies, environment variables, and other best practices to ensure that your serverless applications are protected from vulnerabilities.
- **Cost management**: We discussed cost optimization strategies, such as understanding AWS Lambda pricing and optimizing memory usage to stay within budget while maintaining performance.
- **Scaling and availability**: You learned strategies for scaling serverless applications to handle heavy traffic and ensuring high availability, with a focus on using **AWS Step Functions**, **Provisioned Concurrency**, and event-driven architectures.

8. The Future of Serverless Applications and Python

- **Serverless beyond AWS**: We looked at the evolution of serverless computing with other cloud providers, such as Microsoft Azure and Google Cloud, and explored how serverless technologies are advancing to handle microservices and cloud-native applications.

- **Python's role in the future**: You learned how Python continues to evolve for serverless applications, with improvements in runtime performance, the development of new frameworks, and enhanced support for machine learning and AI workloads.

Final Words of Encouragement

Congratulations! By completing this book, you've taken a significant step toward mastering serverless computing with Python. You now have the knowledge and skills to build, manage, and optimize serverless applications on some of the world's leading cloud platforms. However, the world of serverless computing is constantly evolving, and staying on top of new trends, tools, and best practices is key to continuing your growth as a developer.

As you move forward, here are some final tips and words of encouragement:

- **Keep Experimenting**: Serverless computing is still a relatively young technology, and there are always new features, services, and patterns emerging. Continue experimenting with new serverless services and architectures to stay at the cutting edge of development.
- **Embrace Automation**: Automate as much of your development and deployment process as possible. Embrace CI/CD pipelines, Infrastructure as Code (IaC), and other modern DevOps practices to streamline your workflow.
- **Focus on Real-World Projects**: Build real-world projects to solidify your learning and demonstrate your skills to others. Whether it's a personal project or a contribution to an open-source community, hands-on experience is one of the best ways to learn.
- **Stay Curious**: The cloud and serverless space is evolving rapidly, and the best way to keep learning is to stay curious. Keep an eye on the latest developments, try new things, and never stop expanding your knowledge.

With serverless computing and Python, you're equipped to build scalable, efficient, and modern applications that are ready for the future. As you embark on this journey, know that you have the tools and the knowledge to succeed.

Your Serverless Development Journey and Where to Go Next: Resources and Further Reading

The journey to mastering serverless development doesn't stop here. This chapter is dedicated to helping you continue growing your skills by providing **resources** and **further reading** on serverless technologies, Python, and cloud computing. Whether you're looking to dive deeper into serverless concepts, expand your knowledge of AWS, or explore new tools and frameworks, there are countless opportunities to learn and evolve as a developer. Let's explore where you can go next.

Continuing Your Serverless Development Journey

You've now gained the foundational knowledge necessary to develop serverless applications, but the real journey begins as you continue to experiment and build. Here are some practical steps to keep moving forward:

1. Build More Real-World Projects

The best way to solidify your understanding of serverless development is by building more complex, real-world projects. By working on projects that integrate various AWS services and Python, you will improve your skills and learn new concepts.

Examples of projects to consider:

- **Serverless Image Processing**: Use AWS Lambda with S3 to trigger image resizing, format conversion, and uploading to a new S3 bucket.

- **Real-Time Notifications**: Build a serverless system that sends real-time notifications based on database changes or events using **SNS** and **SQS**.
- **Serverless Blogging Platform**: Create a serverless blogging platform using Lambda, API Gateway, DynamoDB, and S3 for storing media files.
- **IoT Data Processing**: Develop an application that processes IoT data streams with **AWS IoT, Lambda**, and **DynamoDB**.

2. Explore Serverless Architectures at Scale

As you grow more comfortable with building basic serverless applications, challenge yourself by creating larger, more complex architectures. Consider using **microservices** or exploring **event-driven** and **data-driven serverless applications**.

- **Multi-function Architectures**: Combine several Lambda functions to create complex workflows. Use AWS **Step Functions** for orchestration and manage different workflows for multi-step processes.
- **Event-Driven Apps**: Develop event-driven applications that respond to changes in data, such as file uploads in S3 or changes in DynamoDB tables.
- **Real-Time Data Processing**: Implement serverless data pipelines that process real-time data using **Kinesis, Lambda**, and **DynamoDB Streams**.

3. Contribute to Open Source

One of the best ways to continue your journey is by contributing to open-source serverless projects. By collaborating with other developers, you will learn new techniques and practices, as well as gain experience with different frameworks and tools.

Some popular open-source projects in the serverless space include:

- **Serverless Framework**: An open-source framework for building serverless applications.
- **AWS Chalice**: A Python-based framework for creating serverless applications.

- **LocalStack**: A fully functional local AWS cloud stack to develop and test AWS applications locally.

Contributing to these projects will help you stay up-to-date with the latest trends, and improve your skills in cloud-native technologies.

Where to Go Next: Resources and Further Reading

To continue expanding your knowledge in serverless computing and Python, consider exploring these resources:

1. Documentation and Tutorials

Reading official documentation is always a great way to deepen your understanding. Here are some key resources for serverless development with AWS and Python:

- **AWS Lambda Documentation**: AWS provides comprehensive documentation for all aspects of Lambda, including supported runtimes, event sources, and integration with other AWS services. This should be your go-to reference for any questions regarding Lambda.
    - AWS Lambda Documentation
- **AWS Serverless Application Model (SAM)**: AWS SAM is an open-source framework that simplifies deploying serverless applications. Dive into the documentation and examples to understand how to manage serverless resources using SAM.
    - AWS SAM Documentation
- **Python Serverless Framework**: If you're working with serverless applications and Python, the Serverless Framework is a popular open-source tool for deployment. Their documentation and guides are great for developers who want to streamline serverless app development.

- Serverless Framework Documentation
- **AWS Documentation on API Gateway**: API Gateway is a vital part of serverless applications, and its documentation covers everything from basic setup to advanced integration patterns.
  - API Gateway Documentation

2. Online Courses and Video Tutorials

There are several online platforms offering in-depth video tutorials, certifications, and hands-on labs that can take your serverless knowledge to the next level:

- **AWS Training and Certification**: AWS offers a variety of free and paid training courses that are perfect for developers looking to dive deeper into serverless computing, Lambda, and other cloud services.
  - AWS Training and Certification
- **Serverless Architectures with AWS (Coursera)**: A great course on Coursera that covers serverless architecture patterns, use cases, and how to implement them with AWS Lambda.
  - Serverless Architectures with AWS
- **Udemy Courses**: Udemy offers a range of serverless courses, from beginner to advanced levels. Courses like "**AWS Lambda and the Serverless Framework - Hands On**" or "**Serverless applications with Python**" are great options to further your learning.
  - Udemy Serverless Courses

3. Books for Deepening Your Serverless and Python Knowledge

Books provide structured learning paths and can be an excellent way to go deeper into specific serverless topics.

- **"Serverless Architectures on AWS" by Peter Sbarski**: A comprehensive book on building and deploying serverless applications with AWS Lambda, API Gateway, DynamoDB, and other AWS services.
  - Serverless Architectures on AWS
- **"Python for Data Analysis" by Wes McKinney**: While not specifically focused on serverless, this book covers Python libraries like Pandas and NumPy, which are frequently used in serverless data processing applications.
  - Python for Data Analysis
- **"AWS Certified Solutions Architect Official Study Guide" by Joe Baron, Hisham Baz, and Tim Bixler**: If you want to go beyond serverless and explore AWS as a whole, this guide is essential for those preparing for AWS certification.
  - AWS Certified Solutions Architect

4. Blogs, Podcasts, and Communities

Keeping up with the latest trends and best practices in serverless computing can be as simple as subscribing to blogs and following community discussions.

- **AWS Compute Blog**: Regularly updated with articles, announcements, and best practices around AWS Lambda and other compute services.
  - AWS Compute Blog
- **Serverless Framework Blog**: A great source for articles, tutorials, and community insights into serverless computing.
  - Serverless Framework Blog
- **Python Serverless Community**: Join forums and Slack communities, like **r/serverless** on Reddit or **Serverless Slack Community**, to ask questions, share projects, and learn from other developers.
- **Podcasts**: Listen to serverless-focused podcasts such as **"Serverless Chats"** or **"AWS Podcast"** to stay updated on trends, new tools, and interviews with industry experts.

The world of **serverless computing** and **Python** continues to evolve, and by continuing to explore new resources, frameworks, and tools, you will remain on the cutting edge of development. Serverless architectures offer unprecedented scalability, efficiency, and cost-effectiveness, and Python is a fantastic language for creating these cloud-native applications.

As you move forward:

- **Experiment** with real-world projects.
- **Contribute** to open-source serverless initiatives.
- **Continue learning** by following blogs, taking courses, and reading books.
- **Stay engaged** with the growing serverless community to share knowledge and experiences.

With your newfound skills and ongoing commitment to learning, you're well-positioned to create high-performance, scalable serverless applications. The cloud-native world is yours to explore—happy coding and best of luck in your serverless journey!

Appendix

In this section, we will provide a collection of useful resources and additional information to help you further your serverless development journey. From useful Python serverless libraries and tools to a glossary of key terms, we aim to make sure you have everything you need to build, manage, and troubleshoot your serverless applications effectively.

Additional Resources and Tutorials

Here are some additional resources and tutorials that will help you deepen your understanding of serverless computing and Python, as well as keep you up-to-date with the latest best practices.

1. Serverless Framework Documentation

The **Serverless Framework** is one of the most widely used frameworks for building and deploying serverless applications. The official documentation provides comprehensive guides, examples, and advanced usage techniques.

- Serverless Framework Docs

2. AWS Lambda Documentation

The official **AWS Lambda** documentation is a great resource for learning how Lambda functions work, their limits, triggers, and integrations with other AWS services.

- AWS Lambda Documentation

3. AWS SAM (Serverless Application Model)

Learn about **AWS SAM**, a tool that simplifies the process of building and deploying serverless applications. SAM is tightly integrated with AWS services like Lambda, API Gateway, and DynamoDB.

- AWS SAM Docs

4. Tutorials on Serverless Applications

These tutorials cover a wide range of topics, from building REST APIs with Lambda to processing real-time data:

- AWS Serverless Blog
- Serverless Computing Tutorials
- Python Serverless Tutorials

5. Python Serverless Community

Engage with the Python serverless community by joining online forums, Slack groups, and events. The community is a great way to ask questions, share ideas, and stay updated on the latest trends.

- Serverless Community Slack
- Serverless Community Forum

Python Serverless Libraries and Tools

Python has a rich ecosystem of libraries and tools that support serverless development. Below are some of the most commonly used libraries and frameworks:

1. AWS Chalice

Chalice is a micro-framework by AWS that allows you to quickly create and deploy Python-based serverless applications. It supports Lambda and API Gateway integration, making it ideal for building REST APIs.

- AWS Chalice Documentation

2. Zappa

Zappa is another popular Python library for deploying serverless applications. It is well-suited for deploying **Flask** or **Django** apps to AWS Lambda, turning traditional web apps into serverless ones with minimal effort.

- Zappa Documentation

3. Serverless Framework (Python Plugin)

The Serverless Framework is a popular tool for defining and deploying serverless applications. It supports multiple languages, including Python, and allows you to manage your Lambda functions and resources with ease.

- Serverless Framework Python Plugin

4. LocalStack

LocalStack is a fully functional local AWS cloud stack that allows you to test your AWS applications locally, including Lambda, DynamoDB, and other services. It helps you develop and test serverless applications without needing AWS resources.

- LocalStack Documentation

5. AWS SDK for Python (Boto3)

Boto3 is the AWS SDK for Python, allowing you to interact with AWS services from within your Python code. It's essential for invoking Lambda functions, managing DynamoDB, and integrating with other AWS services.

- Boto3 Documentation

Glossary of Key Terms

Here are some key terms you will encounter while working with serverless applications:

- **Serverless Computing**: A cloud computing model where developers build and run applications without managing servers. Cloud providers automatically handle the infrastructure.
- **AWS Lambda**: A compute service that allows you to run code in response to events without provisioning or managing servers.
- **Event-Driven Architecture**: An architecture where functions or services are triggered by specific events, such as HTTP requests, database changes, or file uploads.
- **Provisioned Concurrency**: A feature in AWS Lambda that allows you to pre-warm a set number of Lambda instances to reduce cold start latency.
- **Cold Start**: The delay that occurs when a Lambda function is invoked for the first time or after it has been idle, as the function container needs to be initialized.
- **API Gateway**: A fully managed service that enables developers to create, publish, and manage REST APIs for Lambda functions and other backend services.
- **DynamoDB**: A fully managed NoSQL database service from AWS that is often used in serverless applications for high-speed, low-latency data storage.

- **Serverless Framework**: An open-source framework for building and deploying serverless applications. It abstracts away much of the complexity of managing Lambda functions and other AWS services.
- **IAM (Identity and Access Management)**: AWS service that allows you to create and manage users and permissions to securely access AWS services.
- **AWS SAM (Serverless Application Model)**: A framework that simplifies the deployment of serverless applications using AWS Lambda, API Gateway, DynamoDB, and other services.

Common AWS Lambda Errors and How to Fix Them

Lambda functions can sometimes fail due to various reasons. Below are some of the most common AWS Lambda errors and how to fix them:

1. "Task timed out" Error

- **Cause**: This error occurs when a Lambda function takes longer to execute than the allowed timeout period.
- **Fix**: Increase the function's timeout setting in the Lambda console. Also, optimize your code to ensure it finishes within the given time.

2. "Function not found" Error

- **Cause**: The specified Lambda function handler in your code or configuration doesn't exist or is incorrect.
- **Fix**: Check the function handler in the Lambda console or in the **serverless.yml** or **AWS SAM** template and ensure it points to the correct handler.

3. "Access Denied" Error

- **Cause**: This error happens when your Lambda function doesn't have the correct **IAM** permissions to access other AWS resources (e.g., DynamoDB, S3).
- **Fix**: Modify the **IAM role** associated with your Lambda function to grant it the necessary permissions for the resources it needs to access.

4. "Out of Memory" Error

- **Cause**: The Lambda function exceeds its memory allocation, causing it to crash.
- **Fix**: Increase the memory allocation for the Lambda function in the Lambda console. Also, optimize the memory usage of your function by minimizing unnecessary dependencies.

5. "Unsupported Media Type" Error

- **Cause**: This occurs when the **API Gateway** expects a different content type than what was sent in the request.
- **Fix**: Ensure that the **Content-Type** header of the incoming request matches what API Gateway expects.

Frequently Asked Questions (FAQs)

Q1: What is serverless computing?

- **A1**: Serverless computing is a cloud computing model where developers build and run applications without worrying about the underlying infrastructure. The cloud provider manages the compute resources, allowing developers to focus on writing and deploying code.

Q2: Can I use Python for serverless development?

- **A2**: Yes, Python is one of the most popular languages for building serverless applications. AWS Lambda, Azure Functions, and Google Cloud Functions all support Python, making it a great choice for serverless developers.

Q3: What is the difference between AWS Lambda and EC2?

- **A3**: **AWS Lambda** is a serverless compute service that automatically scales and charges you only for the compute time you use. **Amazon EC2** is a traditional cloud compute service where you need to manage the underlying virtual machines (VMs) yourself.

Q4: How do I debug Lambda functions?

- **A4**: Use **AWS CloudWatch Logs** to capture log data and debug your Lambda functions. You can also use **AWS X-Ray** for tracing the execution flow and identifying bottlenecks.

Q5: How do I secure my serverless applications?

- **A5**: Secure your serverless applications by using **IAM roles and policies**, **environment variables**, and **encryption** for sensitive data. Make sure to follow best practices for securing APIs and limiting permissions to the minimum necessary for each Lambda function.

Q6: What are cold starts in Lambda, and how can I mitigate them?

- **A6**: **Cold starts** occur when AWS Lambda initializes a function container for the first time or after a period of inactivity, leading to delays. You can mitigate this by using **Provisioned Concurrency** to keep Lambda functions warm or optimizing your function's code to reduce initialization time.

This appendix provides additional resources to help you continue your serverless development journey, understand key terms, troubleshoot common errors, and access further learning materials. Whether you are looking for tutorials, libraries, or answers to common questions, these resources will support your growth as a serverless developer.

With these tools at your disposal, you are well-equipped to continue building, deploying, and optimizing serverless applications with Python. Keep experimenting, building, and learning, and enjoy the exciting world of serverless computing!

Index

A comprehensive index is a useful reference tool that helps you quickly locate specific topics or terms within this book. Below is an index to guide you in navigating through the content.

A

This index should help you quickly locate specific concepts, services, and best practices related to **serverless development** with **Python** and **AWS**. It covers everything from Lambda configurations to error troubleshooting, and from security practices to scaling strategies. Whether you're revisiting key chapters or diving deeper into a specific topic, this index will be a helpful guide.